GOOD MUSHROOM
BAD MUSHROOM

GOOD MUSHROOM
BAD MUSHROOM

Who's Who, Where to Find Them, and How to Enjoy Them Safely

John Plischke III

st. lynn's press
PITTSBURGH

Good Mushroom Bad Mushroom
Who's Who, Where to Find Them, and How to Enjoy Them Safely
(All You Need to Know About the Wild Mushrooms of North America)

Copyright © 2011 John Plischke III

ISBN-13: 978-0-9819615-8-3

Library of Congress Control Number: 2010937018
CIP information available upon request

First Edition, 2011

St. Lynn's Press . POB 18680 . Pittsburgh, PA 15236
412.466.0790 . www.stlynnspress.com

Typesetting—Holly Rosborough, St. Lynn's Press
Cover Design—Jeff Nicoll
Editor—Catherine Dees

Photo Credits
All photos © John Plischke III

Disclaimer: The author and publisher expressly disclaim any responsibility for any adverse effects occurring as a result of the suggestions or information herein, including the handling or consuming of fungi named in this book.

Printed in China by South China Printing Company Ltd.

This title and all of St. Lynn's Press books may be purchased for educational, business, or sales promotional use. For information please write:
Special Markets Department . St. Lynn's Press . POB 18680 . Pittsburgh, PA 15236

10 9 8 7 6 5 4 3 2

TABLE OF CONTENTS

Picking and eating wild mushrooms can be one of the most rewarding experiences any lover of the out of doors or gourmet cooking can experience. Edible wild mushrooms are many times more delectable than store-bought button mushrooms. Many people believe the taste of Morels tops the list. As you comb the woods and fields for mushrooms, you will likely learn more about the out of doors than you ever felt possible. The experience is like hunting for a treasure chest. It is exciting and fun. However, you need to be aware of potential dangers.

SOME GUIDELINES FOR YOUR HUNT

You will encounter many very nice people. You may also encounter tics, poisonous snakes, bears or wild dogs. Be careful not to break a leg or get lost. Be cautious, but enjoy the hunt. Be exacting in your mushroom identification. Buy several field guides to aid you, and triple check your information. Go hunting with someone who really knows what they are doing. By all means join a mushroom club. If you do, your learning curve will increase dramatically. If you don't know of one, check the North American Mycological Association website at www.namyco.org and find the one closest to you. Remember that any source may

Do you know who's who? One of these can be lethal; the other is a harmless delicacy. (Deadly Galerina on left, Eastern King Bolete on right)

produce a mistake, so cross-check everything. I may even have a mistake in this book, try as I did to make it accurate. It is up to you to triple-check what I say as well.

BEFORE YOUR FIRST BITE

Some people are allergic to chocolate, peanuts or milk; others are allergic to specific mushrooms even though they are edible. The first time you eat a mushroom, eat only a small quantity. Don't eat more than one new type of mushroom at a time. Always thoroughly clean and cook wild mushrooms. Check the field guides to see what they say about alcohol consumption with the mushroom; some mushrooms and alcohol don't mix. You don't eat rotting meat; don't eat rotting mushrooms. Mushroom rule number one is: **When in doubt, throw it out!** Always keep a refrigerated sample (whole, uncooked mushroom) of what you have eaten, which will aid health workers in treating you if you have made a mistake.

IT'S ALL ABOUT ID'ING

This booklet is intended to be a guide to some of the more common edible wild mushrooms and their poisonous look-alikes. It should be only one of the tools you use in identification. Most of the photos in this book have been set up in a way that their use will aid in the mushroom identification process. Some photos show the mushrooms cut in half so you can see how the interior looks or how the cap is attached; others show habitat, plants or trees.

SAFE, NOT SORRY

Although I have picked and eaten wild mushrooms for over 35 years, I always err on the side of caution. As delicious as they may be, they can be dangerous or deadly. The safest thing is not to eat wild mushrooms at all. If you choose to eat them anyway, the responsibility is entirely yours.

That being said, I have one more word for you: Enjoy!

COLLECTING

Basket

Mushrooms can be somewhat fragile, so many folks prefer to collect them in a basket. The first thing to look for when choosing a basket is the direction of the handle. The handle should go from the front to the back of the basket when it is held at your side. It should be connected to the widest ends of the basket, which will make it much easier to carry.

After the basket is purchased it should be stained a quiet color, one that will not make the basket stand out and draw unwanted attention from other mushroom hunters. It should be varnished for protection, which will also make it easier to clean. If you don't have a basket, use a large, clean brown paper grocery bag. I also like to use camouflage netted bags when hunting at a location where the mushrooms need to be concealed because of competition. In addition to mushrooms, in my basket I often keep a field guide, bags, and a small collecting multi-chambered container for delicate mushrooms, as well as a can of mace and a camera. I also like to attach a compass and a whistle to the basket with a piece of string just in case I become lost. Take a cell phone along; you never know when it might come in handy (if you're able to get a signal).

Bags

If you are picking a lot of one kind of edible mushrooms, put them directly into a clean basket. Otherwise, separate different kinds of mushrooms into different bags before putting them into your basket. Wax paper bags are best, but brown paper lunch bags will also do. Do not mix species of mushrooms. It goes without saying that special care should be given not to mix edible and poisonous mushrooms together.

Do not use plastic bags, because moisture and heat build up in them and cause the mushrooms to quickly rot. The main consideration is to always keep mushrooms cool and dry; heat and water hasten the rotting process. When you get home, clean immediately and put the mushrooms in the refrigerator in a paper bag.

Knives

A penknife with several blades is particularly useful in collecting. When I collect mushrooms, I use one with three blades. The large blade is good for cutting edible mushrooms. The smaller blade can be used for digging up the entire mushroom when taking it home to study, since the base of the mushroom will tell you a lot about its identity. Wipe your knife off after collecting a species and make sure to wash it at the end of the day.

After having gotten a whole sample to keep for identification, cut off the rest of the edible mushrooms just a little up from the base. We do this for two reasons. First, so as not disturb the mushroom's mycelium (root system), which may possibly increase the chance of the mushroom reappearing the next year in the same spot. Most mushrooms are like apple trees; if you cut the apple off the tree it does not hurt the tree. The second reason is to keep the mushrooms clean. (See below on cleaning mushrooms)

Walking Stick

A good walking stick is useful in helping you maneuver through rugged territory. It makes us feel a little safer if we come across a poisonous snake or wild dog. It can also be used to push away underbrush and spider webs. Make your own. Get a sapling between 2" and 2½" in diameter, scrape the bark off, and let it dry. Give it a coat of stain, two coats of varnish and you are ready to go.

FIELD CLEANING MUSHROOMS

Cleaning mushrooms begins with picking them. If you just yank them out of the ground and throw them into a basket, dirt will be over everything. That will mean you will have a mess to deal with when you get home. Take your time, cut each individual mushroom off a little above ground level (after identifying it by looking at the base). Do a little field cleaning, knock or trim off the dirt. Pick off that leaf or blade of grass. This will keep the mushrooms relatively clean. Toss out any that are too old, full of bugs, or don't look right. While you are doing this, take another look at each individual mushroom to make sure it is the one you want. Be sure not to pick mushrooms that are too old; leave some for seed (spores).

HOME CLEANING & PREPARING

As soon as you get home, clean your mushrooms again. Cut off any bad spots and throw away any mushrooms that have deteriorated since you were in the woods. I prefer to use a small soft brush to finish cleaning the mushrooms. A little brush here, and a little brush there, and they are ready. Sometimes a little water has to be used in the cleaning process, but this is not the preferred method. Mushrooms may become soggy when soaked in water. Water can also hasten deterioration. Some people won't even pick mushrooms if they are wet from the rain.

When home cleaning, always take another close look at each individual one to be sure you have picked a good, edible one and not a poisonous one. Some mushrooms have hollow stalks and occasionally critters will crawl inside. The solution is to always cut the mushrooms in half from the top to the bottom of the stipe (stalk). All button mushrooms (still closed or not entirely opened) should be cut in half or sliced, so you can see what the inside looks like – you might see the egg shape of a poisonous Amanita when you thought you had a field mushroom! Cutting will enable you to see the gill color, which will aid in identification.

REFRIGERATION

As soon as you are done home cleaning your mushrooms, freeze, dry or marinate them. If you are going to use them fresh, put them into the refrigerator as soon as possible. Place them in clean paper or wax paper bags – never in plastic bags, as that will hasten the spoiling process. Depending on the variety, many mushrooms will keep in the refrigerator for three to four days. If your mushrooms are not refrigerated they will deteriorate at a much quicker pace; the microscopic bugs that are in them will soon develop and ruin the entire lot almost overnight. I repeat, just as you would not eat a rotting piece of meat, don't eat a rotting mushroom.

FREEZING

We try to freeze a variety of mushrooms in the time of plenty so that we can enjoy them throughout the year. Start by cutting up your mushrooms as if you were going to use them fresh. Place them in a pan and cook them in butter, making sure they are completely cooked. Then let them cool slightly so your fingers don't get burned, and place the mushrooms and their liquid into re-sealable freezer bags. The size of the bag and the amount of mushrooms in each should be what you would use for one meal. Squeeze all the air out and seal the bags shut, then (this is very important) label the bags with the date that you froze them along with the quantity and type of mushroom, and put them into the freezer. Most frozen mushrooms look somewhat similar, and it is hard or impossible to tell what variety is in a bag unless it has been labeled. This is particularly true when they are cooked and you have a number of different types of mushrooms frozen. Try to keep all frozen mushrooms together so they don't become lost in the freezer. Throw them away after six months.

To defrost: Set them out in your sink for a couple of hours, or defrost in the microwave by using its auto-defrost feature. Once thawed, add them to your recipe.

DRYING

First, double-check the identity of your mushrooms, then re-inspect them to make sure only fresh mushrooms are used. Cut away any bad spots and worm holes. In summer, mushrooms such as Boletes get worms, which bore from the base of the stem and work upwards. Just start cutting away the base of the stem until you no longer see any holes; if they continue into the cap you will have to discard the mushroom.

How To Dry

One technique is to string the mushrooms with fishing line, then tie the ends of the string to trees, or hang the string full of mushrooms in a hot attic to dry. You could also tie the strings up in front of an oscillating fan. Some people like to dry them in the oven on low heat. The method that I recommend, however, is using a food dehydrator. The mushrooms must be sliced ¼" thick or less in order for them to dry properly. Put them close together on the dehydrator trays, but leave a little space for the air to circulate.

It usually takes about eight hours to dry mushrooms; after four hours in the dehydrator they usually shrink to about 50% of their original size. The mushrooms that are on the bottom shelf or closer to the fan and heat source of the dehydrator dry more quickly than the ones on the top shelf. To speed up the drying process, about halfway through combine the mushrooms on the two trays closest to the heat source and use that empty tray to add any mushrooms not yet dried. Place that tray on top of the stack, then continue to combine the rest of the trays in this manner.

When dry, the mushrooms should be quickly sealed in airtight jars or zipper bags and stored in a dark place so the light won't fade them and leach out their vitamins and minerals. Make sure to label each bag with the improperly canned foods, especially ones that are not acidic. If you are willing to give it a try, contact your local county extension office first. They will have instructions and a list of approved methods.

BEFORE YOU BEGIN TO COOK

First of all, remember to save a few of your uncooked mushrooms just in case you become sick. That will make it much easier to identify what you ate. They should be uncooked and not prepared in any way, and refrigerated to be kept fresh. When the hospital calls, it is very difficult and often impossible to identify the mushrooms someone has eaten by the stomach contents. Also remember that some mushrooms such as the Alcohol Inky can make you sick if any alcoholic beverages are drunk before or after eating them, so be careful.

As I cautioned in the Introduction, if this is the first time you are eating a species, try only a small quantity, since you may be allergic to them even though they are edible. And do not eat more than one type of mushroom at a time; otherwise, you would not know which one you are allergic to if you have an allergic reaction – or in the case of poisoning, it would be too difficult to find out which of the many species that you ate could be the cause of the poisoning.

date, quantity and type of mushroom. You may want to put your dehydrator outdoors in a protected area, such as on a covered porch. (Be aware that some people are allergic to mushroom spores or do not like the odor.)

To re-hydrate

Soak dried mushrooms in hot water or milk for 20 minutes or so, until they become soft. Put them in a bowl and cover them with the liquid. Once they are reconstituted, you can pour off the liquid or use it to make soup, since it has absorbed some of the mushrooms' flavor (use the liquid as you would use fresh mushrooms as you would use fresh mushrooms: 2 ounces dried mushrooms = about 16 ounces fresh mushrooms.

MARINATING

When I marinate I usually use an empty canning jar, or similar jar that I have saved. Then I cut up and cook my mushrooms and add my spices and put everything in the jar. Depending on the ingredients, marinated mushrooms usually keep a couple of weeks in the refrigerator.

CANNING

Mushrooms can be canned but I don't recommend it, because many people have become ill after eating

COOKING MUSHROOMS

As a general rule, all mushrooms should be cooked before eating. If you are a beginner and want to try wild mushrooms and don't know any for sure yet, get some at the grocery store. Today, many of the bigger stores sell button mushrooms and some other cultivated or wild mushrooms such as Shitake, Oyster mushrooms, Wood Ear, Black Trumpets, Morels, Boletes, and Chanterelles — often available both fresh and dried. Other mushrooms such as the Paddy Straw Mushroom and Enoki can be found canned in the Oriental foods section of the store.

If you desire to purchase even more varieties of wild mushrooms than your store carries, contact Fungi Perfecti (see Resources page at the back of the book). They sell over 20 types of mushroom kits that you can use to grow your own "'shrooms," and they'll send you a nice little catalog. Their kits really do work; I've tried several of them.

If you cook your mushrooms in a pan with butter as we often do, occasionally too much liquid will develop in the bottom of your pan (mushrooms are over 90% water). Just remove some of the water so your mushrooms won't become too soggy. Some mushrooms, such as the Abortive Entoloma, taste better if cooked in butter on medium heat until slightly browned (when the juice starts to disappear). Others taste better not browned. Experiment a little.

Chicken Mushroom Cacciatore
(recipe on p. 82)

IF YOU ARE NOT 100% SURE OF THE IDENTIFICATION OF MUSHROOMS, DON'T EAT THEM. REMEMBER THE MUSHROOMER'S SAYING:

"WHEN IN DOUBT, THROW THEM OUT."

BASIC MUSHROOM ANATOMY

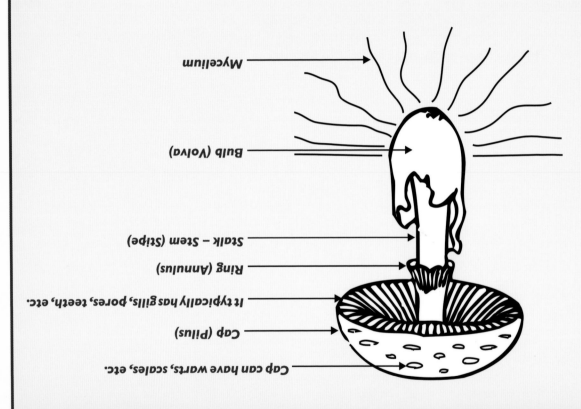

Cap can have warts, scales, etc.

Cap (Pilus)

It typically has gills, pores, teeth, etc.

Ring (Annulus)

Stalk – Stem (Stipe)

Bulb (Volva)

Mycelium

ix

COMMON MUSHROOM TERMS

Bruise – Some mushrooms change colors when they are bruised or scratched, as seen on some species of Boletes and other mushrooms. When the pores get scratched they may change colors (for instance, from yellow to blue). The color changes can vary.

Fertile surface – This refers to the part of the mushroom that is spore-bearing. It could be gills, pores, teeth or veins, and is often on the underside of the mushroom.

Flush – When a quantity of mushrooms quickly appears it is called a flush – for example, if 50 mushrooms appeared under a tree in a yard overnight.

KOH (potassium Hydroxide) test – A drop of 3–5% KOH mixed with water can be applied to parts of the mushroom, such as the cap, and produce a color reaction. For example, a mushroom with a pink cap can change to green where the KOH was applied. Color reactions vary from non-distinctive to distinctive color changes.

Latex – Some mushrooms, especially the Genus Lactarius, produce a substance called latex; when the gills are scratched or the mushroom is broken, this milk-like juice may appear.

Mycelium – This is the collective name for the threadlike structure at the bottom of the mushroom, usually found underground or covered.

Spore Print – A spore print is a deposit of mushroom spores. The color of the spore print can be useful to help determine the type of mushroom and it may also let you know if you may have made a mistake in the mushroom's identification. (See next page for more information.)

Veil – A thin covering over the gills, etc., occurs on some young, immature mushrooms, covering the fertile areas between the cap's outer edge and the top of the stalk. When it breaks apart it can form a ring (a partial veil) on the stalk. Other mushrooms such as Amanitas have a universal veil covering the immature mushrooms; as the mushroom develops and breaks free, a sac-like cup remains at the base of its stalk.

Zones – Many mushrooms can have zoned caps; the zones are often multi-colored in concentric bands on the top of the cap, like rings.

HOW TO MAKE A SPORE PRINT

Why make a spore print? Spore print instructions are not something that authors put into books just to take up space. They can save your life. Different types of mushrooms have many different colors of prints: white, yellow, pink, brown, black and more. The color of a spore print will not tell you what the mushroom is, but it may tell you if you made a mistake in the mushroom's identification. If the mushroom you're ID'ing is supposed to have a white spore print but the print turns out brown, you know you're on the wrong track and there was a mistake in the ID.

To make the print, place a fresh mushroom cap on a sheet of paper with the gills or pores facing down. The stalk may need to be removed or a hole made in the paper to allow for the stalk. It can then be covered with a cup or bowl to stop any harsh air movement from blowing the spores away. The mushroom is left there anywhere from a few hours to overnight. When the mushroom is removed, the print will be left on the paper. It is often preferable to place white colored paper under one side of the cap and black under the other; that way, if it has a white print it would show up on the black paper or if the print is black it would show up on the white paper.

Spore printing an Agaricus

A brown colored Agaricus spore print

xi

INEDIBLE OR POISONOUS MUSHROOMS

BERKELEY'S POLYPORE

(Bondarzewia berkeleyi / Bondarzewia montana)

DESCRIPTION

When immature before the caps develop, it resembles a Gomphus, or a bunch of whitish stalagmites growing up from the ground. When it gets around 6" tall, it should start to look like its mature form. Can get over 3 feet wide but typically about 2 feet wide at maturity, looking like a rosette. Its taste is mild when immature, becoming bitter when fully grown. *B. montana* is also known as *B. mesenterica*.

Flesh: White.

Cap: A caplet is 2½" – 10" wide and ⅛" – 1" thick. *B. berkeleyi:* creamy in color on the upper surface, sometimes with some off-white, yellowish or brownish. Margin sometimes a lighter color. Often zoned. Caplets become fused together on their interior sides and at the base. Overlapping caps in the cap clusters are fan-shaped. *B. Montana:* tannish brown to brownish. It typically is a little smaller and can somewhat resemble an Albatrellus.

Berkeley's Polypore (B. berkeleyi)

Pores: White, becoming cream colored with age and descending down the stalk. Not circular, but somewhat angular and often ridge-like.

Spore Print: White.

Stalk: 2" – 4⅜" tall and 1" – 2 ½" wide. *B. berkeleyi:* creamy to yellowish. Often central. *B. Montana:* brownish. Both species' stalks are attached to an underground tuber-like mass called a sclerotium.

1

BERKELEY'S POLYPORE

Berkeley's Polypore (B. berkeleyi)

WHERE, WHEN HOW TO LOOK

Where: On soil, but connected to wood. *B. berkeleyi* usually grows touching at the bases of hardwood trees, typically oak trees or stumps, but occasionally growing 10 feet or so away from the tree on underground roots. It is more eastern and central in range. *B. montana* is western and grows in the same manner but on conifers such as pine, spruce and fir.

When: July to November.

How they appear: Usually singly at the base of a tree, but sometimes several can be found at a tree.

How common...how rare? Occasional to common.

LOOK-ALIKES

The edible Black-Staining Polypore *(Meripilus sumstinei)*, which differs by bruising black. The edible Umbrella Polypore *(Polyporus umbellatus)*, which differs by having circular caps and a central stalk on each caplet. The edible Sheep Head *(Grifola frondosa)*, which has smaller caps and does not taste bitter or bruise black. All three of the above are edible. The inedible Dye Polypore or Dyer's Mushroom *(Phaeolus schweinitzii)* has flesh that is yellowish to brownish or with rusty tones.

EDIBILITY

Edible but too bitter to be eaten when mature.

2

DEADLY GALERINA
(Galerina marginata)

DESCRIPTION

Galerina mushrooms are typically brownish colored, and for the most part are very difficult to identify to species, many requiring a microscope. It is important to learn about this mushroom because it has been responsible for numerous **poisonings**. Can be mistaken for other mushrooms, including Stump Mushrooms, the Velvet Foot, and Magic Mushrooms. In the recent past this mushroom was called *Galerina autumnalis*. It is from ½" – 4" tall.

Flesh: Creamy to brownish. Much thinner than the gills and usually less than ¹/₁₆" thick.

Cap: ½" – 2½" wide and ⅛" – ⁵/₁₆" tall. Brownish to light yellowish brown with hints or spots of orangish. Typically becomes lighter as it ages or dries out, when tan tones then develop at places. Convex, becoming almost flat with age. Outer edge of its margin can be lined.

Gills: ¹/₁₆" to ¼" deep, and attached to the stalk.

Deadly Galerina on moss-covered wood

Yellowish brown, becoming spore colored as they mature.

Spore Print: Rusty brown.

Stalk: ½" – 3¾" tall and ⅛" – ⅜" wide, and often wider at the base. The partial veil leaves a ring that does not stick out much on the stalk. Stalk gets darker as the mushroom matures. Brownish, but can be whitish at places; also smooth and hollow. Has white colored mycelium that can occasionally be seen when pulled out of loose, rotted wood.

DEADLY GALERINA

WHERE, WHEN & HOW TO LOOK

Where: On rotten wood such as logs usually missing the bark. On both hardwood and conifers.

When: May to December, more commonly, but some all year. Can even be found frozen in December.

How they appear: In small groups to scattered or in larger amounts.

How common...how rare? Common in the U.S. and in eastern and western Canada.

LOOK-ALIKES

American and European DNA collections of both *G. marginata* and *G. autumnalis* have been compared and they are identical, proving they are a single species, now called *Galerina marginata*. This name was chosen because it was published first.

EDIBILITY

Extremely Poisonous. Can cause death. The lucky ones who survive have extended hospital stays and thousands of dollars in medical bills. Two common stories told by survivors of poisoning by this mushroom: 1) *"I thought I could skip the spore printing because it took too long."* If they had taken the time, they would have seen that this mushroom has a rusty brown print and the mushroom that they thought it was had a white spore print; and 2) *"I did do the spore print, but I thought the book was wrong."* When you're dealing with possible fatal poisoning, it's a good idea to trust the book. And always spore print. It may save your life.

FLY AGARIC
(*Amanita amerimuscaria nom. prov.*)

DESCRIPTION

This mushroom gets its common name because it has been used to "kill" flies. In the recent past there were three forms: *Amanita muscaria var. formosa* (yellowish orange capped); *Amanita muscaria var. muscaria* (reddish capped); and *var. alba* (whitish capped). These color forms from the lower 48 states and Canada have now been combined under one name because of DNA testing. The *ameri* was added in front of species *Muscaria* to indicate that ones found in North America differ from ones found in Alaska, Europe and Asia; however, one in the Pacific Northwest appears to be a form of the European ones.

Flesh: White.

Cap: 2" – 12" wide. Convex, becoming almost flat with age. Color forms can be yellowish orange (more common in the East), reddish (more common in parts of the West), or whitish, which is uncommon. Colors often fade some with age. Outer edge has some small lines

Fly Agaric – yellow-orange form

around it. Sticky when wet, and can be shiny. Whitish raised patches or warts on top.

Gills: Free and crowded. White to whitish. Sometimes barely attached to the stalk.

Spore Print: White.

Stalk: 2" – 7¼" tall and ¼ – 1⅜" thick. Whitish but can develop yellowish tones at places. Its universal veil leaves the warts on the cap and on the multiple layers of rings around its roundish, bulb-like base. The rings are one of the keys for ID'ing.

FLY AGARIC

Fly Agaric – red form

WHERE, WHEN & HOW TO LOOK

Where: On the soil under fir, spruce, pine, hemlock, birch, oak – also under madrone, but not often. Typically found under conifers.

When: June to November. California, fall through the winter into spring

How they appear: Singly to in small or extremely large groups. Can be either scattered about or growing in a circle around a conifer.

How common…how rare? Very common.

LOOK-ALIKES

Many Amanitas, including: *A. muscaria var. persicina*, which differs by being peach colored and from the South; the edible but not recommended American Caesar's Mushroom *(A. caesarea)*, which lacks the warts; the edible but not recommended Blusher *(A. rubescens)* and the unknown edibility Yellow Blusher *(A. flavorubescens)*, which bruises reddish at places. The unknown edibility Yellow Patches *(A. flavoconia)* and *A. frostiana* lack the multiple layers of rings above the bulb. The **poisonous *A. gemmata*** has a single moat-like ring above the bulb.

EDIBILITY

Poisonous. Foolish people consider trying it for its ***hallucinogenic*** properties. Some people have mistakenly eaten it, confusing it with an Agaricus, but their trip was not a pleasant one and involved a stay in the hospital. The way traditional medicine men ate it involved first feeding it to their animals to remove some poison and then collecting and drinking the animals' urine! This mushroom should never be used or experimented with.

JACK O'LANTERN
(*Omphalotus illudens and olivascens*)

DESCRIPTION

This mushroom gets its name because when it is taken into a dark room its gills will often glow faintly green once your eyes become adjusted to the dark (in about 5 minutes). This only works when the fungi are mature and fresh. Height is 3" – 9¾". *O. olivascens* has olive-colored tones and grows in western North America. *O. illudens* lacks the olive tones and grows in eastern North America. The dividing line is at about the Rocky Mountains.

Flesh: Light orange.

Cap: 1¼" – 8" wide and ¼" – 1¼" thick. Convex, becoming flat then sunken in the middle with age. Orange to orangish yellow and can get darker colored patches with age. Outer edge becomes wavy or lobed. Margin is inrolled when young then curves up and out at maturity; can be lobed and often splits open with age. Smooth and moist to the touch. Short and broken lines run from the center out. Can have a small raised lump on the top where the stem pushes up

Jack O'Lantern – mature O. illudens

from beneath. With age, shows brownish to blackish patches or spots.

Gills: 1/16" – 5/16" deep, descending partway down the stalk. Orangish yellowish; lighter than the cap.

Spore Print: Whitish cream.

Stalk: 1½" – 8" tall and 3/8" – 1 1/8" thick. Tapers off at the base, becoming narrower. Slightly darker in color at the base; stalks are usually fused together at the base but not always. Smooth, grooved and slightly different in color from the cap or gills. Its lines run from the top to the bottom, as the grooves.

7

JACK O'LANTERN

Jack O'Lantern – young O. illudens in button form

WHERE, WHEN & HOW TO LOOK

Where: Always found on wood. On oak and other deciduous trees, look around stumps, trees; occasionally growing on buried wood such as tree roots, so be careful.

When: In northeast and central U.S. and eastern Canada, July to October. In southern U.S., extending until the end of November. In California, November through March.

How they appear: Usually in clusters.

How common...how rare? Very common.

LOOK-ALIKES

Many of the Chanterelles, such as the following edibles: the Chanterelle *(Cantharellus cibarius)*; Smooth Chanterelle *(C. lateritius); C. californicus; C. formosus* – all of which do not have true gills; they also differ by not growing on wood. The False Chanterelle *(Hygrophoropsis aurantiaca)*, which is much smaller and not found in large clumps and clusters with the stalks fused together at the base.

EDIBILITY

Poisonous. Ingesting this mushroom can cause symptoms varying from vomiting, diarrhea and cramps – to death.

KORF'S GYROMITRA/SNOW MUSHROOM
(Gyromitra korfii / Gyromitra montana)

DESCRIPTION

Until recently, these two mushrooms were considered separate species, with *G. korfii* growing east of the Rockies and *G. montana* west of the Rockies. Testing has now determined that both species are synonymous with the European *G. gigas*, which is the current name.

Flesh: Slightly brittle and whitish.

Cap: 1½" – 4" tall and ¾" – 4¼" wide. Yellowish brown to beige to reddish brown and often lighter; can be colored like the stalk on the underside. Wavy to wrinkled and lacks the sponge-like holes of a Morel. If it looks like a brain. The interior is white and has lots of irregular sized, wavy chambers that go into the stalk; there is not an interior separation of the cap and the stalk.

Stalk: ½" – 2¾" tall and 1" – 3" wide. Whitish or cream colored. The stalk is unusual since it is often wider than tall. Usually wider near the base. When cut, it can bruise very slightly pinkish after a period of time. Can be very wavy, with wrinkles or ribs that tend to run up and down. It is short.

WHERE, WHEN & HOW TO LOOK

Where: East of the Rockies: On the soil in deciduous or mixed woods. Often in Morel woods that have been logged a few years ago with lots of stumps – and near stumps or trees. I have found it under elm, apple and tulip poplar. It can also grow in mature woods. **In the West:** On the soil in the mountains near melting snow. Conifers are often present.

Korf's Gyromitra

6

KORF'S GYROMITRA / SNOW MUSHROOM

When: In the East, April to June 15. In California, in the spring and around August. In the Rockies, varying by elevation.

How they appear: Singly or in small groups. Can be found in larger groups of 30 to 40, but often no more than six are in a group.

How common...how rare? Occasional to common.

LOOK-ALIKES

The edible true Morels, Morchella species, differ by having sponge-like caps and hollow stalks without chambers. The often **poisonous Helvella species**, (those that resemble Morels) usually have a different season. The Conifer False Morel *(Gyromitra esculenta)* has a darker cap and only grows under conifers. The *G. caroliniana* typically has a taller stalk in relationship to the cap and is not as round in appearance. *G. fastigiata, G. infula,* and *G. ambigua* differ by having a more saddle-shaped or lobed cap. *G. sphaerospora* and *G. california* are umbrella-shaped.

Snow Mushroom – also known as Snowbank False Morel

EDIBILITY

Some people can eat Gyromitra, but it is a very bad idea. The **poison** may or may not get you today, but can build up in your system and kill. This one is **poisonous** to some but others can eat it at least for a period of time without a problem if it is well cooked. Mushrooms that might cause problems are never worth eating.

PECK'S MILKY
(Lactarius peckii var. peckii)

Peck's Milky

DESCRIPTION

Peck's Milky is 2" – 4" tall. It does not have a fish-like odor, which sets it apart from the edible and similar-looking Bradley (L. volemus). Its taste is very hot and burning. Tasting is not typically done on inedible fungi such as this one, but if an edible Lactarius description stated "not hot or burning" and you found it to have the hot taste, you could prevent a mistake in identification. Tasting does not mean eating or swallowing; rather, taking a small bite of the cap and rolling it around on the tongue for five or 10 seconds to see if the burning starts, then spitting it out. The hot burning taste of Peck's Milky, and of some Lactarius, can make the mouth and tongue burn for several minutes and be very unpleasant.

Flesh: Often light brownish.

Cap: 1¾" – 5¾" wide. Convex, then depressed and sunken in the middle with age. Zoned. Margin is inrolled when young. Orangish to orangish brown or orangish red.

Gills: Attached to the stalk and a little decurrent (extending downward). Light orangish to orangish brown or reddish brown, or with some rusty tones. They are close.

Latex: Whitish and heavy flowing. Does not change color when flowing.

Spore Print: White.

Stalk: ⅝" – 2½" tall and ⅜" – 1" wide. Orangish to orangish brown or orangish red, often a shade or so lighter than the cap. Occasionally has little roundish spots darker than the rest of the stalk. Becomes stuffed to hollow with age.

PECK'S MILKY

WHERE, WHEN & HOW TO LOOK

Where: On the soil in deciduous woods. Also found by walking down deeply wooded roadsides or semi-wooded park areas. I find it near oak. *Lactarius volemus, corrugis,* and *hygrophoroides* are often found nearby. Mostly eastern in range but also into Texas.

When: July to October.

How they appear: Singly or in groups to scattered.

How common...how rare? Occasional to common.

LOOK-ALIKES

The edible and delicious Corrugated Cap Milky *(Lactarius corrugis)*, which differs by not being hot-tasting and by smelling like fish. The edible, delicious Bradley *(L. volemus)*, which differs by not being zoned on the cap; it smells like fish and does not taste hot. The edible and delicious Hygrophorus Milky *(L. hygrophoroides)*, which does not smell like fish and does not taste hot. The *L. deliciosus* group, which differs by having orange latex and its flesh stains green. The **poisonous Yellow Latex Milky** *(L. vinaceorufescens)*, which differs by having white milk

The Corrugated Cap Milky, an edible look-alike that can be found nearby in some areas

that turns yellow. The **poisonous** Woolly Milk Cap *(L. torminosus),* which differs by having a woolly or hairy-looking cap. Orange Russula *(Russula sp.),* which differs by not having milk. *L. peckii var. glaucescens,* which has white latex that turns green when dried, and is southern. The latex of *L. peckii var. lactolutescens* differs by being white, then light off-yellowish, then greenish.

EDIBILITY

Unknown, but too hot to be eaten.

PIGSKIN POISON PUFFBALL
(Scleroderma citrinum)

DESCRIPTION

Also called Earthballs and False Puffballs. Some companies pay $8 a pound for it for use in inoculating trees to make them more drought resistant.

Mushroom: ½" – 4" wide and 3/8" – 1 7/8" tall. It is yellowish brown with large, rough scales that feel a little like sandpaper. The scales tend to be more brownish and the cracks between them more creamy yellowish. It is leathery and roundish. When mature, typically a single hole or tear develops on the top for spore release. If its skin is scratched the injury can bruise pinkish. When pulled out from loose sandy soil, you may find thread-like mycelium at its base. The Parasitic Bolete (*Boletus parasiticus*) is often found growing from it.

Interior: Inner skin is white, with a thickness of 1/16" – 1/8" or less; it is harder, thicker and tougher than the real Puffballs. Never feels marshmallow-like; much harder than that. The interior, where the spores are,

Pigskin Poison Puffball

starts off whitish when young and small, then turns darker, with the darkening starting from the center outwards, and will become dark purplish to a little darker and almost blackish. Can be a little marbled looking.

Spores: Blackish to brownish black.

PIGSKIN POISON PUFFBALL

Scleroderma cepa, a look-alike

WHERE, WHEN & HOW TO LOOK

Where: On the soil. Typically found in the woods or wooded areas growing under or near trees, such as hemlock, oak, and pine and many others. Look along wood edges. Occasionally it grows on very rotten wood that has fallen to the ground and deteriorated.

When: July through November.

How they appear: Singly to in large groups or scattered. Occasionally 20 or more are found in an area.

How common...how rare? Common. This is the most frequently found Scleroderma.

LOOK-ALIKES

The real Puffballs, which do not have thick and tough leathery skin and are not purple and hard inside when mature. *S. cepa,* which does not have the large rough scales, has a much smoother appearance and can bruise reddish (see photo). *S. areolatum,* which has skin that looks more cracked rather than scaly, and feels smoother. *S. bovista,* which is lighter colored, not nearly as rough, and its skin, which is not as thick, does not resemble sandpaper. *S. polyrhizon,* which when mature develops rays when it opens. *S. verrucosum,* which has a sterile base and typically lacks yellowish tones.

EDIBILITY

Poisonous.

14

RED MOUTH BOLETE
(Boletus subvelutipes)

DESCRIPTION

A note about **poisonous Boletes**: A beginner will be wise to follow the *Bolete rule* and never eat any Bolete that has orange to red colored pores, or any that bruises blue, or any with a bitter taste. By following the rule a few good edibles will be missed but a lot of the poisonous Boletes, like this Red Mouth Bolete, will become excluded, keeping one much safer.

All parts of the Red Mouth Bolete bruise bluish black very quickly and easily, often just by holding it. This is a good example of a Bolete that has orange to red colored pores and one that also stains blue. Although its range is more eastern, I chose it because one of its look-alikes grows in the West.

Flesh: Yellow. Bruises bluish black, then lightens over time.

Cap: 2" – 5" wide. Convex, becoming almost flat with age. It is reddish to reddish orange, with yellow or brown tones. Bruises bluish black.

Red Mouth Boletes

Pores: Orangish to orangish red, but occasionally yellowish near the cap margin. Brownish tones can develop over time. Typically lighter in color than the cap. They are attached and quickly bruise bluish black.

Spore Print: Olive brown.

Stalk: ¾" – 4" tall and ⅜" – ¾" wide. Reddish, but can develop some brownish tones and often has some yellow near the pores. Can have a streaky

RED MOUTH BOLETE

Red Mouth Boletes

appearance. A less commonly encountered form can have some reddish dot-like specks near the top with a more yellowish background color in that area, but colored regularly from at least the middle or so down. It bruises bluish black. The base typically has reddish hairs when fully mature, but they start out yellowish. Best to use a magnifying glass. Does not have any reticulation (network-like pattern), and is solid.

WHERE, WHEN & HOW TO LOOK

Where: On the soil under hardwood trees; more commonly oak, but can also be found under beech and conifers such as hemlock and spruce.

When: June through October.

How they appear: Singly, scattered or in small groups.

How common...how rare? Somewhat common in U.S. and eastern Canada.

LOOK-ALIKES

Boletus discolor=*Boletus erythropus var. discolor*, which differs by having flesh that is not reported to turn whitish after the blue bruising. *B. flammans. B.*

luridus, *B. luridiformis*, and the western *B. pulcherrimus*, which all look very similar. *B. rubroflammeus* is more reddish.

EDIBILITY

Poisonous.

SCALY VASE CHANTERELLE
(Gomphus floccosus)

DESCRIPTION

Also called the Woolly Chanterelle. Some people consider the genus to be Turbinellus. It is 3" – 7" tall.

Flesh: Thick and whitish.

Cap: 1 3/8" – 5½" wide. Orangish red to orangish or orangish yellow, and has scales. Vase-shaped to trumpet or funnel-shaped. Its margin is wavy or lobed, and whitish to creamy yellowish. Western ones are more reddish while in the East they are more orange.

Fertile Surface: The sides are wrinkled to veined and descend down the stalk. Whitish to yellowish. Its veins can be forked.

Spore Print: Ochre.

Stalk: 1½" – 4" tall and ½" – 2" thick at the top. Wider at the top, getting thinner going down. Whitish to yellowish, becoming hollow with age.

Scaly Vase Chanterelle

WHERE, WHEN & HOW TO LOOK

Where: On the soil under hemlock and in mixed woods under evergreen trees.

When: Fruiting June through September in most areas, but in California from the fall through February.

How they appear: Singly to scattered or in small groups.

How common...how rare? Found occasionally.

17

SCALY VASE CHANTERELLE

LOOK-ALIKES

The Pig's Ear Gomphus *(G. clavatus)*, which differs by being purplish to purplish gray on the underside. The **poisonous *G. kauffmanii***, which has a somewhat brownish cap. The **poisonous *G. bonarii***, which does not get red and does not have bright orange colors; a recent research paper considers it to be the same species as *G. floccosus*.

EDIBILITY

Poisonous to many; should never be considered for the pot.

Scaly Vase Chanterelle

SMOOTH THIMBLE CAP
(Verpa conica)

DESCRIPTION

It is smooth and thimble- or bell-shaped; hence, the names.

Cap: ³/₈" – 1 ¼" tall and ³/₈" – 1 ¹/₈" wide. Thimble-shaped, becoming bell-shaped. Ranges from light to dark brownish on the outside. When turned inside out, the part of the cap nearest the stalk is cream to tan colored. Attached to the stalk only at the very top, not in the middle or base. Skirt-like. Bottom and sides are not attached to the stalk and just hang free. Smooth; can be somewhat wavy or folded, but not wrinkled.

Flesh: Thin and brittle.

Stalk: 1 ⁵/₈" – 2 ½" tall and ¼" – ⁵/₈" wide. White to yellowish tan or cream. Stuffed with whitish cottony fibers and can have chambers, or cross ridges, but becomes partly hollow with age (it is variable). Somewhat brittle, smooth, and slightly granular. Can break when you try to cut it in half. Wider near the base, getting narrower going up towards the cap.

Smooth Thimble Cap

Typically it is taller than the cap. Can look like it has brownish stretch marks similar to a person who has had a big weight change.

WHERE, WHEN & HOW TO LOOK

Where: On the soil in deciduous woods. Under elm, in old dying abandoned apple orchards. The typical orchard habitat has been overgrown with trees standing 20 feet taller than the apple trees, and the old apple trees are now scattered throughout the woods.

SMOOTH THIMBLE CAP

Under crabapple and wild cherry, but not nearly as common. Often found growing near Morels.

When: April to May, about the time apple trees are in blossom in the East. They are found on the West Coast winter to spring, depending on elevation.

How they appear: Singly to scattered. Sometimes in a small group.

How common...how rare? Occasional.

Wrinkled Thimble Cap – a look-alike

LOOK-ALIKES

V. digitaliformis (if in fact a different species) differs by its cap having lots of small, closely-spaced pits. The Wrinkled Thimble Cap *(V. bohemica)* differs by having a wrinkled cap (see photo). The edible Half Free Morel *(Morchella semilibera)* differs because its cap is half attached to the stalk and it is sponge-like. Other Morels *(Morchella sp.)* all differ by having the base of their caps attached to the stalk. They also differ by being sponge-like. **Poisonous** *Gyromitra sp.,* has wrinkled brain-like to saddle-shaped caps, many of which are connected to the stalk at the base.

The **poisonous** *Helvella sp.,* those that resemble Morels, are saddle shaped or lobed and do not have the sponge-like holes; and usually have a different season.

EDIBILITY

Not recommended.

VISCID VIOLET CORT
(Cortinarius iodes)

DESCRIPTION

The biggest genus of gilled mushrooms is Cortinarius, with more than 1000 species. Corts get their name because they have a cortina (or "curtain") that resembles a spider web covering the gills on immature mushrooms whose caps have not fully expanded. The cobweb-like covering soon disappears.

Viscid Violet Cort is also called the Spotted Cort.

Flesh: Lightish or with lilac to purplish tones.

Cap: $7/8'' - 2\frac{1}{4}''$ wide. Convex, becoming less so with age. It is purplish, fading or sometimes being lilac. Can be sticky or a little slimy when it's wet out, but dry to the touch when in the sun for a while or just dried out. Smooth, but can have several colored spots, creamy tan to more often yellowish.

Gills: Attached to the stalk and closely spaced. They start off lighter than the cap color and can have violet tones, but with age become darker than the stalk, with rust colors. Can be covered with a cobweb-type veil before the cap fully expands.

WHERE, WHEN & HOW TO LOOK

Where: Under deciduous trees such as oak.

When: July to October in the East. In California and the West, into at least December.

Viscid Violet Cort

Spore Print: Rust or rusty brown.

Stalk: $1^3/8'' - 2^7/8''$ tall and $1/4 - 3/8''$ wide. Wider near the base. Can have purplish streaks, but be whitish in other areas. Sticky when wet and moist, but can become dried-out by the sun.

21

VISCID VIOLET CORT

Cortinarius violaceus – a look-alike

How they appear: Single to scattered or in small groups.

LOOK-ALIKES

The Slimy Violet Cort *(C. iodeoides)*, which differs by having spores that are not as wide and a bitter taste if one touches their tongue to the cap. Don't try licking the cap however; it should be only done by advanced collectors (I have yet to encounter someone who has identified *C. iodeoides* based on licking the cap). *C. violaceus*, which is darker and deep purple, as is the stalk and cap (see photo).

EDIBILITY

Although it is edible, it is not recommended. It does not taste good and Cortinarius has many **poisonous** species in its group (see photo). It is important to learn the features of this genus. Only one species, *C. caperatus,* the Gypsy Mushroom (formally known as *Rozites caperata)* is commonly collected for the pot by experienced mushroom hunters. They grow on the soil, typically under some type of tree. Spore print color is rust to rusty brown, or with a brown tone.

Morels Stuffed with Crabmeat
(recipe on p. 80)

EDIBLE MUSHROOMS

ABORTIVE ENTOLOMA
(Entoloma abortivum)

DESCRIPTION

This Entoloma is a gilled mushroom that attacks and deforms (aborts) another, darker colored, gilled mushroom, the edible Stump Mushroom (*Armillaria*). In the middle of the photo opposite, the roundish mushroom is the aborted form, the result of the Stump Mushroom having been aborted. The aborted form smells like cucumber or bread dough or wet flour.

Entolomas in the aborted stage take on two types of forms: The most common is ½" – 4" wide and ½" – 2" tall. Sides are uneven and somewhat irregularly rounded. Can be cracked and indented in the top center, like a brain. Underneath is often a little stalk. When viewed upside down the area around the stalk appears a bit sunken, like a moat around a castle. Whitish, often with pinkish tones at places. When cut in half it is a little marbled. Feels soft and slightly spongy. The second form is shaped like a balloon that has been stretched out by pulling on the top and the knot; typically taller than wide (can be 2" – 5" tall

Armillaria (left), regular form aborted form Armillaria (center), Entolomas (right)

The **un-**aborted, regular Entoloma is 2" – 4¼" tall. Its description is below.

Flesh: White.

Cap: 1" – 4⅜" wide. Convex, becoming almost flat to slightly sunken or nipple-like in the middle with age.

and 1" – 3" wide), often with raised streaks running from the top down. Top area is typically wider than the base.

ABORTIVE ENTOLOMA

Often has an inrolled outer edge. Whitish gray to grayish brown and smooth. Often coated with pink spores.

Gills: Crowded and descending down the stalk a little. Light gray, but becoming pinkish as the spores mature.

Spore Print: Pinkish.

Stalk: 1" – 4" tall and ¼" – ¾" wide, getting wider going down the stalk. The same color as the cap and sometimes slightly lighter. The mycelium of both aborted and un-aborted stages is white and string-like.

Abortive Entoloma – tall form

WHERE, WHEN & HOW TO LOOK

Where: On loamy, loose soil in deciduous and mixed woods, by fallen and rotten logs, and often by oak trees – and where the edible Stump Mushroom *(Armillaria)* can be found. Occasionally grow 3 feet up a stump, often growing in the same spot for years.

When: August to November

How they appear: In groups that can be touching at places, fused at the base and somewhat at the sides; but can also be scattered. Often a full bag can be collected at a good spot.

How common...how rare? Occasional to common.

LOOK-ALIKES

Beginners should not eat the un-aborted form even though it is edible; it is too easy to make a mistake and confuse it with other, **deadly**, types of **Entoloma**.

EDIBILITY

Edible and delicious, breaded with eggs or lightly browned in butter with garlic and olive oil. Eat only the firmer ones. Soggy-to-spongy ones are too old; push on the tops to tell.

ALCOHOL INKY
(*Coprinopsis atramentaria*)

DESCRIPTION

Many of the mushrooms that used to be known as Coprinus (aka Inky Mushrooms) in our favorite field guides are regrettably not called Coprinus anymore. This can make it harder for beginners to determine which of the four groups the mushroom belongs in. DNA testing has split the group apart, leaving Coprinus but adding Coprinellus, Coprinopsis, and Parasola. But there is still some debate on what goes where. Most people think of Coprinus as a summer to fall mushroom, but it and some species, including the Shaggy Mane, the Mica Cap, and Coprinus Romagnesianus, appear in the spring during Morel season; earlier in the year, the Shaggy Mane is only found in small numbers.

Flesh: White to cream when fresh, occasionally with faint pinkish tones. It turns grayish right before the mushroom starts turning inky. Flesh is not as thick as the gills.

Alcohol Inky

Cap: 1" – 2⁷⁄₈" wide and 1" – 3" tall. Bullet-shaped, turning bell-shaped or convex with age. Its margin is incurved when immature. Color is gray to grayish brown or grayish tan. When immature, it often has a whitish scaly area in places, then larger, darker, more brownish, scaly-looking areas near the cap center when it matures – the center area typically being the scaliest. The skin can peel to the slight knob on the middle of the cap. Eventually turns to ink, starting at the outer edge and working towards the cap's center.

ALCOHOL INKY

Gills: Up to $7/16$" deep. They are free, crowded, and often touching. Color is whitish, turning sometimes faintly pinkish, then grayish, then black, and then to ink.

Spore Print: Black.

Stalk: $1\frac{1}{2}$" – 6" tall and $\frac{1}{4}$" – $\frac{3}{4}$" wide; fibrous when pulled apart. The veil can leave a faint mark on the lower part of the stalk. White, with gray to brown areas, and hollow.

WHERE, WHEN & HOW TO LOOK

Where: On the soil in lawns, where there are usually no living trees present. They can be growing on buried wood or buried mulch or surface mulch. Or around stumps or roots between a sidewalk and curb, where trees have been cut down a couple of years earlier.

When: In the East, central region and Pacific Northwest, May to October. In California, October through April. All year to a lesser extent if in warmer, wet locations.

How they appear: In groups or clusters that are often touching at places.

How common...how rare? Common.

LOOK-ALIKES

The edible Mica Cap *(Coprinus micaceus)* and the edible Shaggy Mane *(Coprinus comatus)*.

EDIBILITY

Edible, but use with caution. ***Warning:*** Alcohol should not be consumed 48 hours prior to or after eating this mushroom or you can become very sick. It contains a compound called Coprine, similar to Antabuse, with ill-effects lasting up to 5 days. With the warning in mind, it is good cooked in scrambled eggs. Discard the stalk before cooking, since it can be a little tough and woody. Surprisingly, this mushroom can be dried in a food dehydrator.

BEAR'S HEAD TOOTH

(*Hericium americanum*)

EDIBLE

DESCRIPTION

There are four *Hericium* that are commonly encountered in the United States and Canada. Unlike many mushrooms that have some type of cap with teeth underneath, these are just teeth that can have small branches. All four species of them are delicious edibles if collected before they turn yellowish and become bitter. *Hericium* are now cultivated and can occasionally be found in the grocery store.

Bear's Head Tooth is typically 4" – 12" wide and 5" – 22" tall; however, there are rare exceptions where enormous amounts can be found covering a large part of a fallen tree trunk, extending eight or more feet along the trunk. Its numerous branches hold the teeth.

Flesh: White and can be brittle. Becomes creamy, then yellowish with age.

Teeth: ½" – 1½" long. Teeth are in small groups on a fungal branch, with a good many groups of teeth forming the mushroom. The teeth come to a point at the end, pointing towards the soil.

Spore Print: White.

Stalk: Having a stalk is not typical, but occasionally it can be found somewhere under the bark and be up to 2" long if pulled out of well-rotted wood. Any part sticking out of the bark would be very small and hardly noticeable.

Bear's Head Tooth

BEAR'S HEAD TOOTH

Bear's Head Tooth in pan

WHERE, WHEN & HOW TO LOOK

Where: Typically found on dead hardwood logs (with or without bark), and less commonly on living trees. Look on maple and beech, also oak and other hardwoods. Eastern and central in range, and western Canada. Look on trees that have become split by lightning or have wounds (which seem to be more commonly infected).

When: August to October.

How they appear: Usually singly, but sometimes several can be found on a log or group of logs.

How common...how rare? Found only occasionally.

LOOK-ALIKES

The edible and choice Comb Tooth *(H. coralloides)*, which has smaller teeth, $1/8$" – $3/8$" long, and grows on hardwoods. The edible and choice Bearded Tooth or Lion's Mane *(H. erinaceus)*, which has much longer teeth, $3/4$" – over 2" long, looks like a beard and has no branches. *H. abietis*, which grows on conifers such as fir and hemlock from Northern California through the Pacific Northwest. The Bear's Head Tooth and the three other Hericium look-alikes are fairly distinctive, and are in a safer group. Not so with **Coral Mushroom**s, some of which can be **poisonous**. Corals typically have branches that face upwards, not downwards, as Hericium. Corals should be avoided until one learns which are edible and which are poisonous.

EDIBILITY

Edible and delicious. Only eat the fresh young ones that are white. Once it starts to turn creamy yellow it becomes bitter. Hericium are great in seafood dishes.

BLACK TRUMPETS

(Craterellus fallax/Craterellus cornucopioides)

DESCRIPTION

Black Trumpet is one of the very best edible mushrooms; also called Horn of Plenty. Can be hard to spot since it blends in well with the soil and leaves. Shaped like a funnel or trumpet, it is $3/8" - 3^3/16"$ wide and $1" - 5^1/2"$ tall. Its margin is usually blackish, inrolled and fairly even, becoming wavy to somewhat lobed and uplifted with age, when it can also become split. Sunken top is gray brown to brownish black or blackish and can have little raised flecks on it. Can smell a little fruity.

The fertile surface is smooth to vein-like with wavy looking vertical ridges, and often with depressions. Outer surface is grayish to grayish brown to brownish black, or blackish to orangish, or salmon to orangish brown, or orangish gray, and can have a little pinkish. It bruises somewhat blackish.

Flesh: Thin and colored like the top, to darker. Can be a little brittle and is easily damaged if piled high during collecting or bumped around in a paper bag.

WHERE, WHEN & HOW TO LOOK

Where: On the soil under mixed woods or deciduous trees such as oak, beech and hickory – 95% of the time under oak or beech – in either semi-open or fully

Black Trumpet

Spore Print: Ochre to pinkish buff or orangish or salmon, for C. fallax. White for C. cornucopioides.

Stalk: If it has one, it is small and cap colored.

BLACK TRUMPETS

wooded environment. Most often found in moss but also in leaf litter with no social plants (ones in leaf litter often twice the size of ones in moss).

When: In most areas, the end of June to October. California, late fall through February. Large flushes often occur at the end of June if there have been two-plus inches of soaking rain; without it, the crop will be a lot less productive.

How they appear: In clusters or small groups to scattered.

How common...how rare? Occasional to common, often in large numbers.

LOOK-ALIKES

A creamy yellow form called *C. konradii,* which is found in the West in places like California. *C. cinereus* (sometimes called Black Chanterelle), which has a long, distinctive stalk and does not resemble a trumpet or vase as much. Fragrant Black Trumpet *(C. foetidus),* which has a long stalk and is eastern in range. The Blue Chanterelle *(Polyozellus multiplex),* which grows under conifers.

At a grocery store near my house, one can purchase a package of 6 Black Trumpets for about $7. How much do you think these are worth? Shown here covering two paper shopping bags.

EDIBILITY

Edible and delicious.

EDIBLE

BLEWIT
(Lepista nuda)

DESCRIPTION

Also called *Clitocybe nuda*. A white inedible mold, *Harziella capitata*, can develop on Blewit gills.

Flesh: Thick and light violet.

Cap: 1½" – 5⅜" wide and convex, becoming almost flat; can get a little sunken in the center. Its margin is inrolled when young but as it matures, can become wavy to lobed, then sticking upwards. Purplish violet but can fade to tannish brown. Moist and can be slippery when wet but will not have slime on it. Does not have a veil.

Gills: Crowded and notched by the stem. Light purplish to violet, but lighter in color than the cap. Can fade with age, becoming more tannish.

Spore Print: Pinkish to pinkish buff.

Stalk: ⅞" – 3" tall and ⅜" – 1¼" wide – wider going down the stem. Stalk is lighter than the cap but has some violet-purple; develops tannish tones when it ages or fades. It is tough.

Blewit – Note the cap colors:
purplish when young, brownish when older

WHERE, WHEN & HOW TO LOOK

Where: Last year's leaf piles are a prime location – somewhere shady. Look in parks and find out where they dump their fall leaves. Occasionally found on grass and compost piles; sometimes grows in fairy rings. Look in the woods along small, narrow creeks that have a hill on either side with giant oak trees (often near housing plans where the land is too steep to build on). Occasionally found under conifers such as pine and in older, untreated mulch; and under other tree types.

BLEWIT

When: August through November. In most areas often after frost or when colder weather brings on peak fruiting. In California, from November to early May.

How they appear: Singly to scattered, or in small groups. Usually in good numbers.

How common...how rare? Common.

LOOK-ALIKES

Purple colored Corts *(Cortinarius sp.)*, many of which are **poisonous**, including the similar **Silvery-Violet Cort** or **Silvery Cortinarius** *(C. alboviolaceus)* shown in photo, and the **Viscid Violet Cort** *(C. iodes)*. Cortinarius differ by having rusty brown spore prints, and for a short period of time (when they are young) they can have a cobweb veil on their gills, but it disappears with age. Other Lepista or Clitocybes such as *C. saeva, L. glaucocana, L. irina,* and *L. graveolens* are not as purple as *L. nuda* when fresh and non-faded. *Clitocybe gilva=L. gilva =L. flaccida* has a cap that is dull-orangish. *L. martiorum's* cap can be orangish or occasionally with purple but not deep purple shades. The edible *L. tarda* is a little smaller and thinner-fleshed.

The similar-looking C. alboviolaceus – a poisonous Cortinarius, one of many

EDIBILITY

Edible and delicious. Typically the stalk is too tough to be eaten. Excellent served with peas.

BRADLEY
(*Lactarius volemus var. volemus*)

Bradley

DESCRIPTION

Also called Saffron Milk Cap, Fish Milk Milky, and Voluminous Latex Milky, it is 2" – 6" tall. When mature it smells like fish but when in the button stage the odor is often not present.

Flesh: White, but bruises or turns brownish; slightly fragile.

Cap: 2" – 5⅜" wide. Convex, becoming almost flat with age and can become indented in the center to funnel shaped. The margin in younger specimens is inrolled; with advanced age it can become upturned. Orange to orangish brown. The middle of the cap is often slightly darker in color. Not zoned; smooth to slightly wrinkled.

Gills: Attached to the stalk and can descend if a little. Closely spaced. White, becoming creamy colored with age. They stain brown when cut or if bruised after a little time. Can be forked.

Latex: White at first. Its flow can be very heavy. If the stalk gets cut, the milk can often entirely cover the cut area. It will make your fingers sticky and stained. It stains the mushroom brown.

Spore Print: White.

Stalk: 2" – 4¼" tall and ¼" – 1¼" wide. It is fairly even, but just below the soil level it gently rounds inwards. Orange to orangish brown and can stain brown when bruised or with aging. Usually somewhat lighter in color than the cap. It often becomes hollow.

BRADLEY

WHERE, WHEN & HOW TO LOOK

Where: In deciduous and mixed woods it is found growing on the soil, often along wooded roadsides and paths. Typically found under larger oak trees.

When: July to September in the eastern and central regions and the eastern Gulf through Texas.

How they appear: Singly or in groups to scattered.

How common...how rare? Occasional.

LOOK-ALIKES

Lactarius volemus var. flavus, which differs by having a yellowish-toned cap and stalk; its range is southern U.S. The edible and choice Corrugated Cap Milky *(L. corrugis)*, which has the same habitat and season. Its gills also stain brown. Has a much more corrugated cap that often has more of the corrugated wrinkled look near the margin. Its cap also has more red. The edible and choice Hygrophorus Milky *(L. hygrophoroides)*, which differs by not smelling like fish. Its gills are widely spaced and also differ by not staining brown when cut. It too has the same habitat and season. The **poisonous Peck's Milky** *(L. peckii)* whose reddish cap and gills dramatically differ by tasting very bitter and hot. The cap differs by being zoned. It also turns brown when bruised, and has the same habitat and season. *L. luteolus* differs by having a lighter colored cap, often with yellowish tones.

EDIBILITY

Edible and delicious.

EDIBLE

CANDY CAP
Lactarius rubidus

Candy Cap

DESCRIPTION

Perhaps the most fun mushroom to collect in the West. In the East there are a few very similar looking and smelling species. Candy Caps have a mild (but never hot) taste and the odor of maple syrup — or maybe brown sugar, burnt sugar or butterscotch. The odor may be very faint to unnoticed in fresh collections, but becomes very distinct when dried. This mushroom has gone by the name *L. fragilis var. rubidus*. Some of its look-alikes differ by having a hot or peppery taste. Tasting does not mean swallowing; rather, either cutting the mushroom and tasting the flesh or latex with one's tongue or taking a small bite and rolling it around on the tongue for 5 or 10 seconds to see if the burning starts, then spitting it out. Some Lactarius can make the mouth and tongue burn for several minutes.

Flesh: Thin and fragile.

Cap: ¾" – 2⅜" wide. Convex, becoming more flat with age. Can be sunken in the center with a small raised area there. Margin is incurved when young but can become wavy and lifted upwards with age. Orangish to orangish brown or a little bit cinnamon in color, occasionally with some reddish tones at places. Not zoned.

Gills: Attached to the stalk and can descend down it a little. Creamy yellow, light orange or light cinnamon, sometimes with pinkish tones.

Latex: Like water and never yellow; or like white cow's milk.

Spore Print: Whitish buff or with faint pinkish tones.

CANDY CAP

Stalk: ¾" – 3" tall and ³/₁₆" – ½" wide. Orangish to orangish brown, or colored like the cap. It is typically both hollow and fragile.

WHERE, WHEN & HOW TO LOOK

Where: Typically on the soil in mixed woods in the West. Not reported in eastern or central U.S. or Canada.

When: January to March in California.

How they appear: Singly or in small groups to scattered.

How common...how rare? Occasional to common.

LOOK-ALIKES

It depends on where one is hunting. *L. xanthogalactus,* of unknown edibility, has a faintly zoned cap, white latex that turns yellow very fast, and sometimes a hot to peppery taste; it is western, but in the East there are two very similar Lactarius that get yellow latex. Of uncertain edibility, *L. camphoratus* and *L. fragilis* var. fragilis have the maple syrup-like odor. *L. rufus* has white milk and a hot to peppery taste that can develop slowly. The western *L. rufulus* is larger in size. There are **poisonous** species of Lactarius, so caution should be used at all times.

EDIBILITY

Edible and delicious. Often used in cookies and on carrots, dessert toppings or made into a flavored oil. If Candy Caps cannot be found locally, a commercial flavored oil is a good alternative. See the Resources page at the back of the book.

CAULIFLOWER MUSHROOM
(Sparassis crispa & Sparassis herbstii)

DESCRIPTION

S. herbstii is from 3" – 12" wide and 3" – 10" tall. *S. crispa* is a little larger and has a large root at the base, which *S. herbstii* does not. These mushrooms can look a little like a head of cauliflower or like a ball of egg noodles. *S. crispa* looks more like egg noodles while *S. herbstii* looks more like a carnation flower top, more flat and less squiggly. They are roundish except at the base. White to cream, turning yellowish at past maturity. When looking down at one in nature, it is covered entirely with numerous leaf-like branches. Each of the branches looks somewhat different in shape and in the amount that they are squiggled or flattened. The leaves start getting fused together about half way or more down to the base.

Flesh: White, becoming creamy.

Spore Print: White.

Stalk: None.

Western Cauliflower Mushroom –
S. crispa

WHERE, WHEN & HOW TO LOOK

Where: In the woods. *S. crispa* is found on the soil at the bases of conifer trees such as pine, while *S. herbstii* is found at the bases of larger oak trees. This mushroom can be found growing in the same place year after year. It is best to cut the mushroom, not to pull it out, leaving a little bit of the base so the mycelium is not disturbed. This will help it to come

CAULIFLOWER MUSHROOM

back again and again in future years. It will also make the mushroom much easier to clean since the dirt on the base is left behind.

When: In the East, July to October. In the West, September through November.

How they appear: They are usually found singly, but on occasion a few can be found together at the base of a larger tree.

How common...how rare? In western North America, *S. crispa* is occasional. In the East, *S. herbstii* is occasionally found, but *S. crispa* is seldom seen.

LOOK-ALIKES

The edible and not as common Umbrella Polypore *(Polyporus umbellatus)*, which has caps that grow on central stems. The edible and choice Sheep Head *(Grifola frondosa)*, which is much darker in color in the brown or gray tones. The edible Black Staining Polypore *(Meripilus sumstinei)*, which is much darker in color in the brown tones and stains black with bruising and with age.

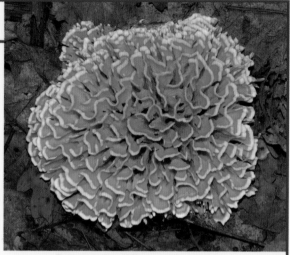

Eastern Cauliflower Mushroom – S. herbstii

EDIBILITY

Edible and delicious.

CHAGA
(Inonotus obliquus)

DESCRIPTION

Also called the Clinker Polypore and Birch Canker. Chaga is also used by natural dyers to dye wool a beautiful yellow color.

It is 2" – 17" tall or wide, but very irregular. Forms can vary a good deal: it can stick out over a foot and resemble a horn, it can stick out a few inches but expand over a larger area, or it can be more rounded, like a ball cut in half. Exterior is black but can have brownish tones. Typically has lots of deep cracks that can cover its surface, looking like it's been scorched by fire. The tree will look like it has a tumor. Interior is often golden yellow but can be brownish at places or rust colored. When fresh it can be cork-like inside but when older it becomes very hard.

Flesh: Corky to hard and typically very thick.

Stalk: None.

WHERE, WHEN & HOW TO LOOK

Where: On both living and dead trees, from ground level to over 30 feet up. It grows on birch 99% of the time, and on a number of other trees, including alder, beech and elm. But only the mushrooms collected from birch are used as tea or medicinally.

When: All year. Typically, Chaga is a more northern mushroom, growing in the northern half of the U.S. into eastern and western Canada.

How they appear... Singly to several; can be scattered on a tree or group of trees.

Chaga

CHAGA

How common...how rare? Uncommon, if there are not birch in the area; occasional to common when birch are in good number. The larger and older the tree the greater the chance of finding it.

LOOK-ALIKES

The Black Knot of Cherry *(Dibotryon morbosum)* = *(Apiosporina morbosa)*, which often grows on cherry branches, deforming them. Looks similar but is not yellowish inside and the host tree is different. Other types of knots often do not look burnt.

EDIBILITY

Can be made into a delicious tea. To make Chaga tea, break the Chaga into ½" or smaller pieces with a hammer. Use both the interior and exterior. Grind the pieces with a coffee grinder until it resembles a powder. Dry the ground Chaga and put into airtight mason jars for long-term storage. To make the tea, add up to a spoon of powder to a cup of boiling water and simmer for 20 minutes. Alternatively, the powder can be used in lesser amounts and added to favorite store-bought teas or coffee to make them "medicinal."

Chaga Tea

This mushroom has also been used in some parts of the world, such as Russia, as a cure for cancer. Others use the tea for arthritis.

CHANTERELLE
(*Cantharellus cibarius*)

DESCRIPTION

From 1" – 3½" tall. A favorite of gourmet chefs.

Flesh: White to occasionally faintly yellowish. Thick.

Cap: ½" – 5⅝" wide and ³/₁₆" – ½" thick. Convex, becoming almost flat; inrolled margin. As it ages, margin becomes upturned, wrinkly, wavy, lobed and irregular. At maturity, often slightly sunken in the center. Roundish to oval and smooth; orangish yellow, almost like an egg yolk. Can smell like apricots.

Fertile Surface: Doesn't have true gills, but ridges or veins that descend part way down the stalk and branch and fork on the outer edge of the cap. Can be cross-veined. It is lighter colored than the fresh cap.

Spore Print: Creamy to light yellowish.

Stalk: ¾" – 3" tall and ³/₁₆" – 1³/₈" wide. Circular but often oval-ish and smooth. Often narrower at the base but can be even or wider at the base. Yellowish orange; can bruise a little darker orange.

WHERE, WHEN & HOW TO LOOK

Where: On soil under many tree types, especially hardwoods such as oak, and conifers such as hemlock. They usually come back in the same spot for years. Found in the middle of the woods or in semi-open wooded areas, cemeteries, parks, picnic areas. Look for some grass underneath. In a good spot you can fill a cooler and more.

Chanterelle

CHANTERELLE

When: In eastern North America, the very end of June to September. In the Northwest, but not into Canada, September to November. In some parts of California, November to February. Season varies in other areas.

How they appear: Seldom singly; more often scattered or in small groups. Typical collecting spot is an area about 70 x 30 feet, with 100-plus Chanterelles.

How common...how rare? Common in the U.S. and eastern Canada.

LOOK-ALIKES

Similar sized and shaped edible Chanterelles include: the eastern Smooth Chanterelle *(C. lateritius)*, which has less distinct, smooth veins; *C. cibarius var. amethysteus*, which has amethyst tones, especially on the cap; *C. cibarius var. roseocanus* of the Pacific Northwest and Rockies, which grows under conifers such as spruce (gills can be more orange than the cap or stem and more eye-catching). In California there is *C. californicus*, which grows under live oaks, less commonly other oaks; in the Pacific Northwest there is *C. cascadensis*, which grows under hemlock and Douglas fir and has a more yellowish cap and somewhat whitish veins. The western Pacific Golden Chanterelle *(C. formosus)* can have pinkish tones and fine scales on its cap. The edible Lobster Mushroom *(Hypomyces lactifluorum)* is a mold that grows on white Lactarius and Russula species. **Poisonous look-alikes** include: the **Jack O'Lantern** *(Omphalotus sp.)*, which has definite gills, grows on wood and is usually much larger (when fresh it will glow in a dark room)...the **poisonous Scaly Vase Chanterelle** *(Gomphus floccosus)*, which has a scaly top and can cause digestive problems...and the **poisonous False Chanterelle** *(Hygrophoropsis aurantiaca)*, which differs by having true gills instead of ridges.

EDIBILITY

Edible and delicious.

EDIBLE

CHICKEN MUSHROOM
(*Laetiporus sulphureus*)

Chicken Mushroom

DESCRIPTION

There are now seven species of chicken mushroom in North America (also called Sulfur Shelf). Its taste and texture are similar to chicken if cooked in chicken broth. Its bright orange color will jump right out at you, making it an ideal mushroom to road hunt. Often a grocery bag or so can be collected.

Flesh: ¼" – ⅞" thick. White to lighter yellowish. Soft and thick.

Cap: Fan-shaped. A single piece of the cap is 2½" – 11¾" wide and ½" – 1" thick. Top is almost fluorescent orange to bright orange, then orangish with age, continuing to fade. Outer edge or margin can be yellowish, becoming wavy to lobed with age. Often fused together at the back. Can be zoned.

Pores: On the underside of the cap. Fluorescent yellow, becoming duller yellow and lighter with age.

Spore Print: White.

WHERE, WHEN & HOW TO LOOK

Where: In the Northeast and the central states, and into Canada. Grows on deciduous wood, typically large oaks but also tree types such as cherry, maple and poplar. Does not grow on conifers. More often on dead trees than living ones. Can reoccur in the same spot for several years. Look on tree trunks both fallen and standing, and on larger fallen branches. When they are growing very high up in a tree, too far to reach, a telescoping pole can be useful for knocking

CHICKEN MUSHROOM

L. sulphureus on a huge log

them down. Be aware that other Laetiporus grow on conifers and eucalyptus and can cause trouble (see Edibility, below).

When: May to October, more common in fall.

How they appear: Typically in single groups or in shelf-like, overlapping clumps. Occasionally found on larger trunks, sometimes covering entire trunks.

How common...how rare? Common in the U.S. and eastern Canada.

LOOK-ALIKES

The edible *L. cincinnatus = L. sulphureus var. semialbinus,* which differs by being white to creamy colored underneath at the pores; caps more pinkish to orange. Typically grows in a rosette at hardwood tree bases (such as oak) in the eastern and central states. The **presumed poisonous L. conifericola,** which grows on conifers in the Pacific Northwest and California; yellow pores. *L. huroniensis,* which grows on conifers such as hemlock; yellow pores also, but grows in the Great Lakes region. *L. gilbertsonii,* which grows on eucalyptus and oak in the West; yellow pores and often salmon colors on top. *L. gilbertsonii var. pallidus,* which grows on oak and perhaps eucalyptus in the Gulf States area; pores are off-white or with tannish and dull tones. *L. persicinus,* which grows on both conifers and deciduous trees in the southeast U.S.; pores are pinkish tan and the top has brownish tones.

EDIBILITY

Edible and delicious as a chicken substitute. Excellent breaded. Best to cut only the tender tips. **Warning:** Laetiporus growing on eucalyptus are **poisonous**. Laetiporus growing on conifers have caused numbness of the tongue in some people who ate them.

EDIBLE

FIELD MUSHROOM
(Agaricus capestris)

DESCRIPTION

Also called the Meadow Mushroom and the Pink Bottom; related to the Button Mushroom (*Agaricus bisporus*) from the grocery store. 1" – 4" tall. Edible, but some similar-looking mushrooms are **poisonous**; it is important to know the difference. Does not stain yellow in Potassium Hydroxide - KOH.

Flesh: White. Occasionally stains slightly pink when bruised or from prolonged rain.

Cap: 1" – 4" wide and ⁵/₁₆" – 1 ¼" tall. It is globose, then convex, becoming almost flat. Whitish, with some cream, brown and gray. In the button stage, edges curl down, and the white partial veil obscures the gills when immature. On some well-matured older specimens cap edges curl up. Skin peels back from outer edge to about the middle of the cap. Smooth, soft, slightly fibrous. Can have some markings or be somewhat wavy.

Gills: Depth about ¹/₈" – ⁷/₁₆". Crowded and free at maturity but slightly attached when immature. Light pink when young, then bright pink, turning brown with age and black with rot.

Field Mushroom

Warning: When gill color is hidden by the white partial veil in the button stage, a mistake can be made by picking a **poisonous** look-alike that does not have the pink to brown gill color of the Field Mushroom.

Spore Print: Brownish black and chocolate.

Stalk: 1" – 2⅜" tall and ¼" – ½" thick. White, sometimes turning slightly pinkish when cut or bruised. Has a small fragile ring growing around it, which sometimes gets washed away with rains or just disappears. Does not have a volva but can taper near base. Usually slightly smoother above the ring than below. Can be solid or stuffed.

FIELD MUSHROOM

WHERE, WHEN & HOW TO LOOK

Where: On the soil in grassy areas, not woods. Look in yards, mown fields, cemeteries, pastures, golf courses, meadows. Occasionally in cultivated fields. Often appear in the same locations for years. Cut any unopened ones in half to make sure you don't get any with white gills; those may be **poisonous** look-alikes.

When: August through September, sometimes into October. Best time: when it starts to cool after a hard long rain. Small quantities sometimes found in late spring. In warmer parts of California, can be found most of the year in wet weather.

How they appear: Usually in small groups to great quantities. Rarely singly. Sometimes in fairy rings.

How common...how rare? Common.

LOOK-ALIKES

The edible Horse Mushroom *(Agaricus arvensis)*, which differs by being larger and bruising yellow. The edible Sidewalk Mushroom *(A. bitorquis)*, which has a double-edged ring on the stalk. The Smooth Lepiota *(L. naucina)*, which has white gills and spore print.

Sink full of Field Mushrooms

Amanita species, most of which are **poisonous**, have a bulb or sac at the base of the stalk and gills, with white spore prints. Two of the many **poisonous Agaricus** *(A. californicus* and *A. xanthodermus)* turn yellow with KOH.

EDIBILITY

Edible and delicious. Stronger and much superior flavor than store-boughts.

GIANT PUFFBALL
(Langermannia gigantea)

DESCRIPTION

The Giant Puffball is a giant, white, roundish, ball-shaped mushroom. 6" – 25" wide and about as tall. When found in a group of three that are touching, the two small ones can be as little as 3½" tall and 5" wide; the large one will be as big as a basketball or larger and can weigh up to five pounds.

Does not have gills or pores. The skin is about 1/16" thick and can be peeled off in big sections with your fingers. If really dirty, it can be field cleaned by peeling off any dirty skin so the dirt does not spread all over them. Its smooth skin becomes cracked with age and often has small dimple-like holes on the surface, probably where some insect had been chewing. Make sure to cut it off at the base; never pull it off the ground, so the mycelium is not disturbed. When pulled from the ground, occasionally a small amount of white, thread-like mycelium remains attached to the base in an area about the size of a quarter.

Flesh: White when fresh.

Spores: White, then turning greenish yellow, sometimes with a little brown. A single one of these mushrooms has millions of spores.

Stalk: None.

WHERE, WHEN & HOW TO LOOK

Where: On the soil in open and open-wooded areas. Look in cemeteries, fields, meadows, parks, pastures, roadsides, yards and grassy areas. Occasionally

Giant Puffball (L. gigantea=calvatia)

GIANT PUFFBALL

at the edges of 20-or-so-foot wooded slopes near roadsides. They are easier to spot if the area has been mowed. A trick to collecting fresh specimens is to gently push down on the top and if it feels firm, it's often perfect. If it feels soft, pushes in easily or feels mushy, it's too old to eat.

When: August through October, usually coming up in spurts. You might collect at five different spots one week, then nothing anywhere for several weeks.

How they appear: Singly, or in small groups to scattered; occasionally in fairy rings. Average collection at one location is one to three mushrooms.

How common...how rare? Somewhat common in the U.S. and eastern Canada.

Giant Puffball acting cool

LOOK-ALIKES

When road hunting for mushrooms, you might spot big, white round things growing in someone's yard... and then be disappointed to find that it's only a soccer ball. Using binoculars to check can save a lot of walking. The edible western Giant Puffball *(Calvatia booniana)*, differs by having lots of raised polygonal shaped areas, like mountains on a relief map. The edibles Skull Shaped Puffball *(C. craniformis)*, Purple Spored Puffball *(C. cyathiformis)*, and *Calbovista subsculpta*, are all softball-sized when mature.

EDIBILITY

Edible and delicious. Eat the pure white fresh ones only. Once it starts getting yellow or darker inside it is rotting; never eat it.

HEMLOCK VARNISH SHELF
(Ganoderma tsugae)

DESCRIPTION

The Hemlock Varnish Shelf and its more famous cousin *Ganoderma lucidum* can be made into a delicious tea with reported medicinal properties. The Hemlock Varnish Shelf is reported to be slightly stronger medicinally. When younger, its upper cap skin will crack like a crab or lobster claw.

Flesh: Whitish and up to 1 ¼" thick and flexible.

Cap: 2½" – 14" wide, sticking out 2" – 11"; fan-shaped and zoned. Top and stalk appear to be varnished and can be very shiny. When smaller and immature it is often reddish brown near the stalk or where connected to the wood, then reddish going outwards, then yellowish orange and finally whitish near outer edge and margin. You could also occasionally see reddish orange, orangish brown, or mahogany. Becomes darker as it matures, more reddish brown to mahogany. Small 1-inch ones are soft but become hard once they grow to a few inches.

Hemlock Varnish Shelf

Pores: Whitish when fresh and up to ½" thick. 4 – 6 per mm (1 mm=.04"). They bruise, then age brownish.

Spore Print: Brown.

Stalk: 1" – 5⅝" long and ⅜" – 1½" wide, but stalk is sometimes absent. Typically grows off to the side where it attaches to the tree, but its placement can also be underneath the cap and vary there. Varnished-looking and typically reddish brown or darker, like the cap.

HEMLOCK VARNISH SHELF

WHERE WHEN & HOW TO LOOK

Where: Typically on dead conifers, usually hemlock and rarely on spruce, fir or pine. Eastern and central.

When: May to December.

How they appear: Singly to in shelf-like groups.

How common...how rare? Common in the U.S. and eastern Canada.

LOOK-ALIKES

All of the following mushrooms can also have varnished-looking caps and have been made into tea. DNA testing may eventually combine or split species of these varnish shelfs: *G. oregonense*, which differs in range by growing in the West on conifers such as Douglas fir, fir, pine and hemlock. Its color is very similar and is reddish brown. An extremely large 3-foot specimen has been recorded but that size is not typical; it is also often thicker. Its pores are 2 – 3 per mm. The Ling Zhi also called Reishi *(G. lucidum)*, is typically found on maple, less so on oak and chestnut. *G. curtisii*, is a typically southern species and lighter colored. *G. resinaceum*, looks almost identical and

Ganoderma tsugae Tea

grows on birch, oak and other trees with leaves instead of needles.

EDIBILITY

Some people eat the tender buttons, but once mature it is too hard for anything except making tea. A few mushrooms will make gallons of tea. Cut into inch-sized pieces, add to boiling water and simmer for one hour. Can be diluted and honey or brown sugar added for a sweetener. Long used in Chinese herbal medicine, it is thought to aid the immune system.

KING BOLETE

(*Boletus edulis*)

DESCRIPTION

This is the most famous of all the Boletes. You may have seen Boletes used on one of your favorite cooking shows, where these mushrooms are called Cep, Porcini, or Steinpilz.

Flesh: White and meaty; it does not stain or bruise blue.

Cap: 2" – 12"-plus wide. Convex, becoming almost flat with age. Somewhat smooth. It is yellowish tan to yellowish brown to reddish brown, or shades in between, but can vary depending on what part of the country it is found in. It does not bruise blue. Turns orangish with a drop of KOH.

Pores: White, becoming a yellow, then yellow olive to somewhat brownish color with age. Can be sunken like a moat near the stalk. They do not stain or bruise blue.

Spore Print: Olive brown.

Stalk: 2½" – 11" tall and ¾" – 3½" wide. Can be somewhat even in width or it can be a lot wider at the base. Western collections tend to have much wider stems. Off-whitish to light brownish and solid. The upper area of the stalk has a fine whitish colored reticulation that looks like a net or web pattern.

Eastern King Boletes

KING BOLETE

Western King Boletes

WHERE, WHEN & HOW TO LOOK

Where: On the soil under conifers. Spruce can be productive.

When: June to October. In California, spring to fall.

How they appear: From singly to in small groups or scattered. Sometimes a basket can be filled.

How common...how rare? Uncommon to occasional to somewhat common, depending on the location.

LOOK-ALIKES

The **poisonous** *Boletus huronensis*, which differs by having light yellow flesh that can bruise blue on occasion. The too-bitter-to-be-eaten Bitter Bolete (*Tylopilus felleus*), which differs by being distinctively bitter tasting and its pores turn from whitish to pinkish. There are many Boletes that were once considered to be, or were called, *B. edulis* – too many to be listed here. There are some similar excellent edible ones, including *B. subcaerulescens*, whose cap turns blue then quickly becomes orange with a drop of ammonia – and the Pink Bolete (*Xanthoconium separans*), which has a pinkish cap and stalk (the pink area turns green with a drop of KOH).

EDIBILITY

Edible and delicious. There is a safety rule that has been used with success for eating Boletes. Since there are over 300 species of Boletes in North America, and **some are poisonous**, Bolete identification can be difficult but important. The rule states never eat any Bolete with orange or red colored pores, never eat any Bolete that bruises blueish and do not eat Boletes that taste bitter – that is, unless you are 100 % certain which Bolete you have. There are blue staining Boletes and ones with orange to red colored pores that are edible, but other ones with those features are **poisonous**. By ruling those out the safety factor will be much better.

MATSUTAKE
(Tricholoma magnivelare)

DESCRIPTION

Also known as the White Matsutake, American Matsutake and Pine Mushroom, and by the name *Armillaria ponderosa*. It has an odor that some people find fragrant and others think smells like old gym socks. Matsutake are a commercial product often exported to Japan.

Flesh: Meaty and solid feeling.

Cap: 2" – 8½" wide. Convex, becoming almost flat with age. The outer edge is inrolled when young but can be facing upwards with age. Whitish when immature but soon becomes yellowish with brown or yellowish brown to reddish beige or reddish brown scales.

Gills: Attached to the stalk. Can be notched and are closely spaced. They are white, aging a little darker into the cream shades or with yellowish tones. Can bruise or turn brownish at places with age. When immature they are covered with a whitish partial veil.

Spore Print: White.

Stalk: 1¾" – 6" tall and ½" – 2" wide. It has a ring and, when mature, scales on the stalk going from its ring down to the bottom. Stalk is whitish above the ring, while the scaly areas below can become creamy to reddish beige or reddish brown or with dull yellowish tones. Can be slightly wider in the middle, tapering off to a narrower, roundish base.

MATSUTAKE

WHERE, WHEN & HOW TO LOOK

Where: On the soil under conifers such as Douglas fir and lodgepole pine in the Pacific Northwest, and hemlock or pine in the East. In California, on the soil under pine, madrone and tan oak. In the West they are often hidden under raised piles of needle duff that give them away. Found in northern North America, but most commonly in the Northwest. Western collectors often look for a plant without chlorophyll called the Candystick, aka Sugarstick *(Allotropa virgata)* as an indicator of possible locations.

When: August through October in the East and central states. October through February in the West.

How they appear: Singly to in groups to scattered.

How common...how rare? Uncommon to common. In the Pacific Northwest it is much more frequently found and many commercial mushroom collectors pick it by the thousands.

LOOK-ALIKES

Tricholoma caligata – but only the non-bitter ones, which are good edibles; *T. Caligata* differs by having darker scales, brownish or purplish brown. The edible

Tricholoma caligatum – a look-alike

western *Catathelasma imperialis*, which can have a much wider cap, and does not smell like old gym socks...and the edible *C. ventricosum*, which also does not smell like old gym socks. The **poisonous Amanita smithiana** does not smell like old gym socks, but be warned: its mistaken identification has caused **poisonings**.

EDIBILITY

Edible and delicious.

OYSTER MUSHROOM
(*Pleurotus ostreatus*)

Oyster Mushroom

DESCRIPTION

Flesh: White.

Cap: Usually 2" – 9" wide and about an inch thick. Often smooth and moist when fresh. Outer edge, away from the tree, is inrolled when young and can be somewhat rounded when very young; can become wavy and lobed with age. Can be somewhat flat or sunken in the center. Cap is tan to grayish or grayish brown or brownish (not white to cream, becoming yellowish). Narrower where it is connected to the tree.

Gills: Can descend a little down the stalk. White to whitish to cream, sometimes a little yellow with age. In winter can be grayish. Edges are not serrated or saw-toothed.

Spore Print: White to whitish to buff or lilac.

Stalk: Usually does not have a stalk; when it has one, it is small and off to one side closest to the wood. White to whitish or grayish, and solid.

WHERE, WHEN & HOW TO LOOK

Where: Typically on dead hardwood trees, on stumps, branches, trunks and fallen logs. Also places where they cut up trees that fall on back roads and throw them a little off to the side of the road. Can come back on the tree twice in the same year and for several years. They especially like trees by streams. (If mushrooms are too high up to reach, it's helpful to bring a telescoping pole and tie your knife on the end).

OYSTER MUSHROOM

Oyster Mushroom Kit (see Resource page)

When: Very late fall and winter. But all year if taking *Pleurotus pulmonarius* and *Pleurotus populinus* with it as a complex (see Look-Alikes below). If picking in the winter, go after a thaw and the temperature has been above 32 degrees.

How they appear: Usually growing in shelf-like, overlapping groups and clusters. Can be found in great quantity, occasionally covering entire fallen logs and trunks.

How common...how rare? Common.

LOOK-ALIKES

In the past, it and the first two below were considered a complex of species that grew all year; now, season and color can help differentiate them: *P. pulmonarius* is usually white to tan when mature, but can be grayish brown; found summer to early fall in the East and springtime in the West, typically on hardwoods. *P. populinus* grows on cottonwood and aspen; buff to tan.

Crepidotus species differ by having spore prints that have brown in them. The edible Elm Oyster *(Hypsizygus tessulatus)* = *(Pleurotus ulmarius)*, has a stalk and usually grows on elm; it has yellowish tones.

Lentinellus species and Lentinus species such as the Bear Lentinellus *(L. ursinus)*, have saw-toothed gills; you need to look at it from the side to see the serrated edges. The edible Late Fall Oyster *(Panellus serotinus)*, has a small stalk; cap can be greenish or purplish, then fading to brownish. The **possibly poisonous Angel's Wings** *(Pleurocybella porrigens)* is smaller and grows on evergreens such as hemlock.

EDIBILITY

Edible and delicious. Sold at many grocery stores.

PEAR SHAPED PUFFBALL
(Morganella pyriformis)

DESCRIPTION

In the past this mushroom went by the name *Lycoperdon pyriforme*, but it differs from other *Lycoperdon* in several ways, including DNA and where it grows (on wood, not soil).

Mushroom: ½" – 1 ¾" wide and ¾" – 1 ⁷/₈" tall, and shaped like an upside-down pear. When very young it is whitish, then with age it becomes a yellowish brown color with some white and tan, which is the way it is usually found. It has small granular particles to faint spines on it, but it can still feel rather smooth. At or near the center of the top, it develops a single hole for the spores to release with age. Interior is white, turning yellowish green to yellowish brown or greenish brown with age. The base has white string-like mycelium visible when the mushroom is pulled out of loose, rotted wood. It has a sterile base that is more evident when the insides become much darker and the base darkens to somewhat creamy, but is still much lighter in color than where the spores are forming.

WHERE, WHEN & HOW TO LOOK

Where: It grows on wood, typically on hardwood. Look on fallen trunks and logs, also on dead stumps, which are usually somewhat rotted. Can grow up the base of an oak. The wood can have the bark on it or not. Occasionally the mushroom can be found on the soil, but that is because it is on buried wood. Can also be on mulched paths in the woods.

Pear Shaped Puffballs

PEAR SHAPED PUFFBALL

Pear Shaped Puffballs

When: In the East, July through November. In California, winter.

How they appear: In groups and clusters or large groups. Often over 100 can be picked on a large fallen trunk or mulched paths. Some are typically touching at places. It can be found singly but rarely. You can expect to find enough to flavor a dish.

How common...how rare? Common to very common. Can typically be found on the same log for several years.

LOOK-ALIKES

The edible Gem Studded Puffball or Devil's Snuffbox *(Lycoperdon perlatum)*, which differs by growing on the soil, not wood. The Spiny Puffball *(L. echinatum)*, which grows on the soil and has distinctive spines. Be aware that there are also other Puffballs that have the spines. *Morganella subincarnata* differs by lacking a sterile base and being a little spiny. Spines disappear with age. It is somewhat pinkish.

EDIBILITY

Edible and delicious. Only eat them when they are white inside and make sure to cut them in half to check that there's not any sign of its being a **poisonous Amanita Button**, which will show faint signs of gills and a cap developing inside. They (not the Amanita Button) are good cooked in butter with chopped up potatoes or breaded. Also excellent in puffball potato pancakes.

SHAGGY MANE
(Coprinus comatus)

DESCRIPTION

It also goes by the name Lawyer's Wig.

Flesh: Thin and white when in prime condition, turning sometimes pinkish but then always grayish, then black as the mushroom ages and turns to ink.

Cap: 1¾" – 8½" tall, more typically to 6". 1" – 2" wide before the base of the cap expands as it turns to ink, becoming up to 3 inches wide. Cylinder-like with rounded top to elongated oval-like shape. Mostly white to whitish and shaggy; the center part of the top of the cap can be tannish to tannish brown, smooth and a little shiny. When maturing, small pinkish tones may develop near the grayish areas, starting near the bottom as the cap turns inky. It is covered with shaggy white scales that can become darker with age. Cap starts turning to ink from the bottom up, becoming shorter as it drips away. Once the sides of the cap are gone, a flat-ish, quarter-sized (or so) area can be still attached to the stalk's top, which can curl upwards.

Shaggy Mane

Gills: Crowded to closely spaced and when mature, free. Whitish, turning sometimes pinkish at places, then always becoming grayish then black and inky with age, dissolving working upwards, as in the cap.

Spore Print: Black.

Stalk: 2" – 10½" tall; more typically up to 7" – 8" tall and ⅜" – ¾" wide. Widens going towards the bottom of the stalk. Whitish and fibrous. Interior is about one-third hollow and can be somewhat cottony.

SHAGGY MANE

Partial veil leaves a faint ring or mark near the bottom. Cap covers and hides most of the stalk.

WHERE, WHEN & HOW TO LOOK

Where: One of the better mushrooms to road hunt for. In yards and other grassy areas, often along or near roadsides, near the bases of huge, aging leaf compost piles. They usually return in the same spot for years.

When: Main flush: September to October. May to June in lesser quantities. In warmer regions, around January or throughout the year at rainy times. Look in the morning; the sun on hot days often turns them to ink by noon.

How they appear: Can be scattered or in small groups or clusters. If you are lucky, 500 or more can be found in a yard.

How common...how rare? Common.

LOOK-ALIKES

The western and much taller *Coprinus colosseus*, which has a stalk between 14" and 20" tall. The edible (with caution) Alcohol Inky *(Coprinopsis atramentaria)*, which is not shaggy.

EDIBILITY

Edible and delicious. Stalks are too woody to be used. Should be processed shortly after being collected because they typically turn to ink quickly.

SHEEP HEAD
(Grifola frondosa)

DESCRIPTION

Sheep Head (or Sheep's Head or Hen of the Woods) is roundish in circumference with numerous overlapping caps. It can be 4" to 12"-plus tall, 5" – 24"-plus wide and weigh 1 – 50 pounds.

Flesh: White and meaty.

Single Cap: Each cap piece is ½" – 3" wide and ⅛" – ⅜" thick. Caplets grow in irregular-sized clusters and are somewhat circular except where connected. Can be lobed; thicker where connected, getting thinner going towards the outer edge. Stalk attaches to the side. Color is variable, from brown to grayish or beige tones; sometimes top outer edge is whitish.

Pores: White, turning a little creamy then yellowish with age. On the underside of the caps and going part way down the stalk.

Spore Print: White.

Stalks: ½" – 1⅝" long. White, turning cream then yellowish with age. Multiple stalks with many

WHERE WHEN & HOW TO LOOK

Where: At the bases of oak trees 99% of the time. The larger the oak, the greater the chance of its being productive. Very rarely it can grow on wild black cherry, yellow birch or gum. Can be found on the same oak tree year after year and up to 10 years after the tree's death. Also found next to the base of

branches, each attached to one side of a cap, and fused together at the base to form a single stalk-like trunk.

Sheep Head

SHEEP HEAD

Grifola frondosa – favorite tree fruiting

oak stumps. Though a common mushroom, it is easy to miss because it blends in with the brown leaves around it. If you find a young fist-sized one it is often good to leave it and come back in a couple of days when it matures.

When: August through November, but September and October are best. On larger productive trees an additional one can occasionally be produced a few weeks later.

How they appear: One or two are usual but on rare occasions up to 17 can be found growing around a single matured oak.

How common...how rare? Common in the East and many parts of the U.S. and eastern Canada. Many hunters collect several dozen a year, even up to 60 in a season. A personal record is 60 in an afternoon, but that was cherry-picking spots acquired over several years.

differs by having circular caps, central stems, a lighter color, and usually grows on beech. The edible Berkeley's Polypore *(Bondarzewia berkeleyi)*, which has much larger creamish colored pieces of the cap (entire cap can be up to 3 feet wide). It also likes oak but it has a bitter taste when mature.

LOOK-ALIKES

The edible Black-Staining Polypore *(Meripilus sumstinei)*, which differs by bruising black. The edible Umbrella Polypore *(Polyporus umbellatus)*, which

EDIBILITY

Edible and delicious, also medicinal. Great pickled, breaded or in spaghetti.

64

SHORT STALKED SUILLUS

(Suillus brevipes)

Short Stalked Suillus (a herbarium photo)

DESCRIPTION

Also called the Short Stemmed Suillus and Short Footed Suillus. No parts of it bruise blue. Most Suillus, unlike typical Boletes, have slimy caps when fresh. There are exceptions, such as *S. pictus*, whose cap does not get slimy, but the slimy cap is a fairly good thing to be looking for. Most mushroom hunters ignore Suillus, preferring to collect the more famous Boletes. Suillus host trees are typically conifers, and experienced collectors often do not go out hiking to find them; instead they drive in their vehicles and road hunt parks and cemeteries, where large rows of pine and spruce are frequently planted right next to back roads. It's easier to just pull over and begin to harvest the better edible species.

Flesh: White to whitish, turning yellowish with age.

Cap: 1¾" – 4" wide. It is convex, becoming almost flat with age. When small and young the outer edge of the cap can be curved slightly onto the lower pore area. Slimy when fresh, but will become dried-out by

the sun. It is brownish but can have gray or cinnamon tones. With age, it often becomes lighter with tan coloring.

Pores: White, turning yellowish with age.

Spore Print: Cinnamon to brown.

Stalk: 5/16" – 2" tall and ¼" – ¾" wide. Whitish, becoming a little yellowish, often at the top half. It rarely has dots, but when present they are more easily spotted on the upper stalk. Can get wider going towards the base. Solid, not slimy, and does not have a ring.

SHORT STALKED SUILLUS

WHERE, WHEN & HOW TO LOOK

Where: On the soil under pine and occasionally spruce trees.

When: August through November. In California, fall to winter.

How they appear: Scattered but often closely spaced or in groups.

How common...how rare? Common.

LOOK-ALIKES

S. brevipes var. subgracilis, which differs by having a skinnier stalk and pores distinctively yellow. The western *S. pseudobrevipes*, which has a veil. *S. granulatus*, which always has a dotted stalk whose granules can often be felt; its pores can be white then pinkish then yellowish, and the stalk can also be pinkish at places.

Suillus brevipes var. subgracilis – a look-alike

EDIBILITY

Edible and delicious to many people if the skin is peeled off before eating. Some people can develop diarrhea if the skin is not removed from the cap before eating. Even though the slime and the added preparation of removing it can be a deterrent to some, collecting Suillus has its advantages.

STUMP MUSHROOM
(Armillaria mellea)

DESCRIPTION

Also known as Honey Mushroom, Podpinki, and Popinki.

Flesh: White.

Cap: ¾" – 5½" wide and ³⁄₈" – ⁵⁄₈" thick. Convex, becoming almost flat with age. Slimy when wet, but dry in dry weather. Often very faintly hairy in the dry in dry weather. Often very faintly hairy in the middle during dry spells. Honey yellow color; can be darker and more brownish in the center.

Gills: Whitish, attached to and going slightly down the stem. When the fungi are young (the cap not yet expanded), the gills are hidden by a white partial veil until the cap expands, breaking the veil to leave a ring.

Spore Print: Whitish to creamy.

Stalk: 1½" – 6" tall and ¼" – ¾" thick. Usually gets thinner and much narrower at the base, but can be wider when stalks are closely fused together in a clump or cluster at their bases. Tough and fibrous with a whitish ring, which can stick out ⅛" – ½". Either

WHERE, WHEN & HOW TO LOOK

Where: Growing on wood around stumps in large groups and clusters, or at the base of live or dead deciduous trees and buried roots. Ideal spots in many areas are large oak trees with or without bark. Logged areas can be excellent. Its black, string-like, bootlace-looking rhizomorphs are often seen when the bark

Stump Mushroom (A. mellea)

cottony or hollow on the inside. White, becoming grayish to brownish with age; often has a few scattered flecks of raised skin.

STUMP MUSHROOM

falls off a dead tree, indicating that Stump Mushrooms occur in the area.

When: In the far West, variable season, depending on elevation and how far north; December to March is most common. In the East, August to December.

How they appear: Often found in large clumps.

How common...how rare? Common, and often return for several years at the same spots.

Stump Mushroom (A. ostoyae)

LOOK-ALIKES

In the past there was only the Stump Mushroom and the Ringless Stump Mushroom. In recent years they have been split into nine different species, prevalent over different parts of North America, among which are: the edible Ringless Stump Mushroom or Ringless Honey Mushroom *(A. tabescens)*, which differs from the others by not having a ring on its stem. The larger, *hallucinogenic* Big Laughing Gym *(Gymnopilus spectabilis)*, which is orange with a dark-colored spore print. The **poisonous Sulfur Tuft** *(Naematoloma fasciculare)*, which has yellowish green gills that can become brownish, and a purplish brown spore print. The **poisonous Deadly Galerina** *(Galerina marginata)* differs by being smaller and having a brown spore print. The **poisonous Eastern Jack O' Lantern** *(Omphalotus illudens)* is orange on all parts; gills can glow in the dark when fresh, once your eyes become adjusted. The **poisonous Western Jack O' Lantern** *(Omphalotus olivascens)* is orangish as above but can have olive tones.

EDIBILITY

Edible and delicious only if cooked; **poisonous if not cooked**. Caps are excellent sautéed in garlic and olive oil.

EDIBLE

SWEET TOOTH
(Hydnum repandum)

DESCRIPTION

Also called the Hedgehog.

Flesh: White to very light orange, and bruises orangish brown.

Cap: ¾" – 6¼" wide. Occasionally even larger forms are found. Convex, becoming almost flat but sometimes with a slightly sunken center half with age. When young, it has an inrolled margin that can become uneven or wavy with age. Orangish to yellowish orange or a yellowish brown color, and bruises a more deep orange. It is smooth.

Teeth: ⅛" – ¼" long. They can descend a little down the stalk. Similar in color to the cap but can be lighter with more white tones. They bruise orangish.

Spore Print: White.

Stalk: 1" – 4" tall and ⅛" – 1⅜" wide. Can be central but is usually slightly off-center. Yellowish orange; lighter near the cap. Usually lighter colored than the cap. Bruises orangish. It is solid and does not become hollow.

Sweet Tooth – underside showing teeth

WHERE, WHEN & HOW TO LOOK

Where: Growing on the soil in woods and mixed woods. Under conifers and deciduous trees; under hemlock and oak. Look in moist areas. They like leaf litter. Can often be gathered in quantity.

When: July through November. In California, winter to spring, starting around January.

SWEET TOOTH

Depressed Sweet Tooth – a look-alike

How they appear: Singly, but more often in small groups to scattered.

How common...how rare? Found occasionally.

LOOK-ALIKES

The edible Depressed Sweet Tooth or Depressed Hedgehog *(H. umbilicatum)*, which differs by being much smaller and having a belly button-like indentation or hole in the center of the cap. The edible *H. repandum var. albidum*, which differs by being lighter colored and more whitish, with an orangish bruising. The edible *H. rufescens*, which differs by having an orangish brown cap that is darker, smaller, and has spines that do not go partway down the stalk. *H. repandum var. macrosporum*, which differs by having larger spores that go beyond 8um (microns) in size, typically 9 – 10um in length. *H. albomagnum*, which differs by being lighter in color, not bruising and not growing in the Northeast. Chanterelle species, which looks similar from the top but differs by not having little teeth under the cap, rather veins. Hydnellum species and Sarcodon look similar but most are not orange. Albatrellus species differ by being pored and not having the teeth.

EDIBILITY

Edible and delicious. They are good fried in butter.

VELVET FOOT
(*Flammulina velutipes* & *Flammulina populicola*)

DESCRIPTION

Also called the Fuzzy Foot, Velvet Shank, Winter Mushroom and Winter Shank. When cultivated and sold in stores it is called the Enoki, Enokitake or Enokitake; this cultivated form is whitish and does not even resemble the wild version.

Flesh: Thin and typically whitish with some cream or yellowish.

Cap: ½" – 2" wide. Convex, becoming almost flat with age. Sticky to a little slimy and shiny in appearance during wet periods but stickiness typically disappears in prolonged dry periods. Yellowish orange to orangish brown to reddish brown, often having more yellow and/or orange, especially near the outer edge.

Gills: Attached to the stalk or notched. Can be closely spaced. Whitish to creamy or yellowish.

Spore Print: White.

Stalk: ¾" – 2⅜" tall and ⅛" – ¼" wide. Often thinner at the base. Orangish brown or with brown

Velvet Foot (*F. velutipes*)

to blackish tones near the bottom. Upper part lighter in color, often with yellowish shades. Velvety near the base. Tough.

WHERE, WHEN & HOW TO LOOK

Where: Typically on dead trunks and branches. In the East, *F. velutipes* is typically found on dead elm (99% of the time, according to many collectors). In the West, extending at least up to the Rocky Mountains and perhaps into the central states and Canada. *F. populicola* is typically found on trees of the genus *Populus* – poplar and aspen. Velvet foot can also grow

VELVET FOOT

Velvet Foot (F. populicola)

on Alnus, pine, spruce, tulip poplar, and willow. The trees can be standing or fallen but are almost always dead. Can grow on stumps.

When: Fall to spring but most common during the winter months in Indian summers or when the snow melts. Can also be found growing in the snow and can survive the snow and continue to mature during warmer winter periods.

How they appear: In close groups or clusters that are typically touching at places. Often, a fallen log can have multiple groups.

How common...how rare? Occasional to common.

LOOK-ALIKES

The **poisonous Deadly Galerina** (Galerina marginata) differs by having a rusty-brown spore print. **Warning:** Many people have been poisoned by picking it by mistake, then making a second mistake of not spore-printing. There are four forms of Flammulina velutipes: F. velutipes var. velutipes as the description above... and the following: F. velutipes var. lacteal, which has a white to whitish cap and stalk; F. velutipes var. longispora, which has longer basidiospores (a type of mushroom spore); and F. velutipes var. lupinicola, which grows on the wood of the bush lupine (Lupinus arboreus) in California coastal areas. A different species, F. rossica, from the West sometimes has pinkish tones at places.

EDIBILITY

Edible and delicious. Used in Oriental dishes.

72

WINE CAP STROPHARIA
(Stropharia rugosoannulata)

DESCRIPTION

From 2" – 8" tall with a wine colored cap. Very easy to cultivate by collecting mycelium-covered woodchips in the wild and covering them with fresh chips back home so they don't dry out.

Flesh: White, similar in thickness to the gills on mature specimens.

Cap: $3/8$" – 1" tall and from $1^1/8$" – 10" wide. Bell-shaped, then convex to almost flat with age. Dry to somewhat moist and smooth. There can be cracks with age and temperature. Can be shiny when young, with small flecks from the veil going around its outer edge. Skin can peel back to almost the middle of the cap. In younger specimens, caps are deep purple to brownish purple to brownish red; older caps can be similar, or the sun can fade them to dark tan to beige.

Gills: Attached to the stalk and can be notched. Can become wavy. Can be off-white when in button form and gills are still covered. Once cap expands, gills become light purplish gray, then almost purplish black with age. There are often white particles or patches of the veil on the gills. On young, unopened specimens gills are often unseen.

Spore Print: Dark purplish to purplish brown.

Stalk: $1^5/8$" – 7" tall and from $3/8$" – $1^1/8$" wide. On older specimens, stalk's bottom can be wider than the top, and the base swollen. Smooth, but when mature, lines run down it and on top by the gills. Often you can see marks on the very top of the stalk that were made

Wine Cap Stropharia

WINE CAP STROPHARIA

by the gills. There is a thick ring on the upper part; can look like claws. Creamy white color, sometimes with beige or streaks. Not hollow but can be less dense inside. When pulled out of the mulch, often has white thread-like mycelium attached. Can be a little cottony-looking around the underground portion of the stalk.

WHERE, WHEN & HOW TO LOOK

Where: In aged mulch and wood chips, but not much in cypress mulch or pine bark or in freshly chipped mulch.

When: In the East, from April to October, but largest quantities in May and June and September and October, the two main flushes. One spot will often have both flushes so check it twice. In the West, season can go to November.

How they appear: Sometimes found singly to somewhat scattered, but typically in large quantities, fairly closely spaced. Often found by the hundreds.

How common...how rare? Common.

LOOK-ALIKES

It can have an uncommonly found whitish-colored form. Several different Agrocybe species can grow in mulch and even beside the Wine Cap, such as the Spring Agrocybe *(Agrocybe praecox)*, which has somewhat brownish gills that are never purple. Wine Cap also looks slightly like an Agaricus, but Agaricus have free gills, often pinkish, turning brown. Numerous other Stropharia and similar-looking Leratiomyces species have caps that vary in shades other than wine.

EDIBILITY

Edible and delicious. Mild flavored. Use as Agaricus.

YELLOW MOREL
(*Morchella esculenta*)

DESCRIPTION

Usually 2¼" – 12" tall.

Flesh: Thin and can be a little brittle.

Cap: 1" – 6" tall and ¾" – 3" wide or wider. Shaped like a conical bullet with a rounded tip. Cap is typically about twice as tall as it is wide. Light tan to yellowish or yellow brown, and can sometimes be darker in the pits with age or drying. Can become orangish in a few little spots. It resembles a sponge and is a darker color than the stalk. The pits are usually taller than they are wide: ⅛" – ¾" tall, ⅛" – ½" wide and ⅛" – ½" deep. Pits and ridges are very irregular in shape. The base of the cap is connected to the stalk.

Stalk: 1¼" – 5" tall and ½" – 2½" wide. Not as wide as the cap where they connect, nor as tall. The wall of the stalk is not very thick. White to cream; lighter in color than the cap. Hollow. Can be granular. Hollow, often becoming a little wider going towards the base.

Yellow Morel

WHERE, WHEN & HOW TO LOOK

Where: On the soil under apple trees (Malus) and in old abandoned apple orchards. The apple trees have to be dying or at least partially dead. Ideal locations: orchards that have turned into woods with other species of taller trees crowding them out. Currently harvested orchards are not typically productive. Also, look under dead and dying elms infected by Dutch elm disease. Morels can appear for several years after the elm has died. Tulip poplars are also productive trees.

YELLOW MOREL

Occasionally, Morels grow under ash, hawthorn, beech, cottonwood, sycamore, oak and fruit trees, such as cherry or pear, and in old burned areas. In some parts of North America, they can be found under alder and evergreens.

When: April through June in the East, but typically only a two month season, which is affected by location. This Morel grows across North America but seasons vary. Picked in February in parts of California.

How they appear: Typically found singly to scattered or in small groups. Larger elm trees and western burns can occasionally produce windfalls.

How common...how rare? Occasional or common.

Field of Morels – all Morels are hollow and lack cotton or chambers on the inside.

LOOK-ALIKES

Other species of True Morels (*Morchella sp.*), which can differ in shape and color but also have sponge-like caps and are hollow inside. The **poisonous False Morels** (*Gyromitra sp.*), which look like a wrinkled brain or are saddle-shaped and lack the sponge-like holes. The **poisonous Thimble Cap Morels** (*Verpa sp.*), which differ by having caps without holes that are attached to the stalk only at the top of the cap. The **poisonous Helvella species** (those that resemble Morels), which are saddle shaped or lobed and are not sponge-like.

EDIBILITY

Edible and delicious. Excellent pan-fried in butter.

Chantrelle Dip
(recipe on p. 79)

Here are 8 of my favorite recipes. You'll find many more delicious dishes using a variety of mushrooms on my web site: http://home.comcast.net/~grifola/site/

Basic Breaded Mushrooms

For this recipe, you can use any of the following mushrooms: Chanterelle, Chicken Mushroom, Field Mushroom, Giant Puffball, Oyster Mushroom, Pear Shaped Puffball, Sheep Head and Yellow Morel.

8 ounces whole mushrooms
2 large eggs
2 tablespoons water
1½ cups Italian or panko bread crumbs

Mix eggs and water in a bowl.

In a second bowl add breadcrumbs. Dip the mushrooms in egg and then in the crumbs. Put into a deep fryer and fry till golden brown.

Serves 6 as an appetizer.

Chanterelle Dip

¾ cup dried Chanterelles
½ cup onion, diced
½ teaspoon garlic, minced
2 tablespoons butter
8 ounces soft cream cheese
Sour cream
Milk

Soak the Chanterelles in enough milk to cover to reconstitute. Then drain and chop fine. Sauté them with onion and garlic in butter for 10 minutes. Cool. Mix with cream cheese, adding enough sour cream to make a smooth consistency.

Serves 10 as an appetizer.

Morels Stuffed with Crab Meat

2 dozen large Morels
1 egg
½ cup breadcrumbs
1 8-ounce can crabmeat
1 tablespoon fresh chives
Salt and pepper to taste

Large *Morchella esculenta* work the best. Use a mushroom brush and clean the Morels. Cut the mushrooms in half lengthwise and set aside. Combine all the other ingredients, except the mushrooms, and mix well.

Stuff the Morels and place them on a non-stick cookie sheet. Bake at 350° F for 15 to 20 minutes.

Serves 4

Puffballs and Potatoes

1½ cups Pear Shaped Puffballs
5 – 6 large red potatoes, diced
¼ cup red and green pepper, chopped
½ cup onion, chopped
1 teaspoon garlic, mashed or chopped
Salt and pepper
Oil

Sauté mushrooms in a small pan for a few minutes, then add rest of ingredients and cook for about 20 minutes or until done.

Serves 4

Mushrooms and Scrambled Eggs

I typically use one of the following: Abortive Ento-loma, Black Trumpet, Chanterelle, Field Mushroom, Oyster Mushroom, Shaggy Mane and Yellow Morel. Use one type.

6 eggs
¼ cup milk
1 teaspoon parsley
Salt and Pepper
¼ – ½ cup Cheddar cheese, shredded
1 cup chopped fungi
Butter

Mix all the ingredients together, except for the mushrooms. Sauté the mushrooms in a pan with some butter for a few minutes, let cool slightly then add the egg mixture to the mushrooms and cook.

Serves 2

Chanterelles and Liquor

Chanterelles
Vodka, Tequila or Schnapps
Ball canning jars and lids

Fill each canning jar to the top with fresh cleaned Chanterelles, then top off the jar with one of these liquors, or a favorite of yours. Better not to mix liquors. Let your preserved mushrooms sit for at least a week so the flavor can be absorbed. During this time your fungi may shrink and you may keep adding additional mushrooms. Make sure to keep your jar(s) in a dark location so your mushrooms do not fade. I keep mine in the back of the refrigerator. Both the liquor and the mushrooms can be used. I am not sure if the liquor improves the mushrooms or the mushrooms improve the liquors' flavor. You will have to be the judge. Enjoy!

Serving size: 1 – 2 mushrooms per person as an appetizer.

Makes about 10 servings, depending on the size of the jar.

Sheep Head Pierogi Pizza

2 square pizza crusts
3 pounds of red potatoes
3 large onions, sliced
Dried Sheep Head, sliced
4 cups cheddar cheese
2 cups mozzarella cheese

¼ cup parsley
Butter
Salt and pepper
Milk, if needed

Dice potatoes and boil until tender, then mash (can add a little milk, if they are too thick). Sauté onions and set aside. Re-hydrate dried mushrooms in hot tap water for 45 minutes, and drain. Sauté mushrooms with parsley, salt and pepper, then add to potato mixture. Spread on pizza crusts, top with the sliced onions, then the cheddar and mozzarella cheeses. Bake 15-20 minutes at 350° F.

Serves 4 – 6

Chicken Mushroom Cacciatore

4 – 6 cups Chicken Mushrooms
1 8-ounce can store-bought mushrooms
1 large onion, chopped
1 green pepper, chopped
½ cup celery, diced
2 14.5-ounce cans diced tomatoes (do not drain)
I small can of tomato sauce size
1 tablespoon Italian seasoning
1 clove garlic, chopped
2 tablespoons parsley
1 26-ounce jar spaghetti sauce
2 14-ounce cans chicken broth

Place the Chicken Mushrooms in a large skillet with chicken broth and cook for about 15 minutes. Drain, then add mushrooms, chopped onion, chopped green pepper, celery, tomatoes, tomato sauce, Italian seasoning, garlic, parsley and spaghetti sauce. Cover and simmer for 45 minutes to an hour. Serve over angel hair pasta or rice.

Serves 4 – 6

ORGANIZATIONS AND PUBLICATIONS

North American Mycological Association (NAMA)
www.namyco.org
NAMA has 70 affiliated mushroom clubs and over 2000 amateur mycologists as members. They offer a 4-day foray each year that 100+ people attend, as well as several regional forays. It's a great way to learn mushrooms quickly. Their bi-monthly newsletter is the *Mycophile*; their annual peer-reviewed journal is *McIlvainea*. Check their web site and find a local club.

Northeast Mycological Federation Inc. (NEMF)
www.nemf.org
It has 18 member clubs and focuses on education. NEMF puts on one of the largest mushroom forays in the world, with attendance from all over the globe. Its 4-day forays take place in northeastern North America and make learning about mushrooms fun and easy.

Fungi Magazine
www.fungimag.com/
Four quarterly issues plus 1 special issue a year

Mushroom: the Journal of Wild Mushrooming
www.mushroomthejournal.com
Four issues a year

PRODUCTS

Fungi Perfecti
P.O. Box 7634
Olympia, WA 98507
Order: 800 780-9129
www.fungi.com
They sell mushroom growing kits, spawn, books and many other mushroom related items.

Oyster Creek Mushroom Company
www.oystercreekmushroom.com
They sell wonderful flavored mushroom infused oils, such as the Candy Cap flavored oil, and a number of types of dried mushrooms.

INDEX

(Inedible or poisonous mushrooms shown in bold)

RECIPES

ACKNOWLEDGMENTS

I wish to thank the North American Mycological Association and the Northeast Mycological Federation and their memberships for providing events that enabled me to learn mushrooms. Thanks to Alan and Arleen Besette, Ursula Hoffmann, Gary Lincoff, Bill Roody, Sandy Sheine, Walt Sturgeon, Tom Volk and all the other mycologists, professional and amateur, who have shared a wealth of information. Thanks to my wife, Kim, for not only tolerating my hobby, but participating in it, especially on our honeymoon! Thanks to my parents, John and Becky Plischke, for encouraging me and taking me to many mushroom events when I was young.

ABOUT THE AUTHOR

John Plischke III has been hunting mushrooms for over 35 years. He is well known throughout the United States and Canada, having given hundreds of mushroom programs to schools, parks, mushroom clubs and many other groups. He is the recipient of more than 80 national and regional awards for his mushroom photography. In 2000, he founded the Western Pennsylvania Mushroom Club with just 14 members. The club is now one of the largest mushroom clubs in the United States, with more than 500 members. John has received the North American Mycological Association's (NAMA) Knighton Service Award.

He is the author of *Morel Mushrooms and Their Poisonous Look A Likes*, has edited the two cookbooks of the Western Pennsylvania Mushroom Club and has been a contributor to many other mushroom books. John is a trustee and faculty member for both NAMA and the Northeast Mycological Federation. He is one of the editors for Fungi Magazine and is chairman of the fungus section of the Pennsylvania Biological Survey.

John can be reached online at: **http://home.comcast.net/~grifola/site/**